EXCELLER
SELECT

TOP PICKS

A Taste of Enlightenment

A Taste of Enlightenment

Exploring the Senses as Gateways to the Soul

Siddharth Kuriyal

EXCELLER BOOKS®
A GLOBAL PRESS

A Taste of Enlightenment
Exploring the Senses as Gateways to the Soul

Cover by Exceller Books using resources from Pixabay.com

ISBN: 978-93-48892-02-7

Published in India in 2025 by Exceller Books,
An imprint of GE Group,
G1, Dream Apartment, Degree College Road, Belgharia,
Kolkata, 700056, India
www.excellerbooks.com

EXCELLER BOOKS®
A GLOBAL PRESS

महामाया महाविद्या भगवती माँ राज राजेश्वरी
भवान्यष्टकम्

न तातो न माता न बन्धुर्न दाता न पुत्रो न पुत्री न भृत्यो न भर्ता ।
न जाया न विद्या न वृत्तिर्ममैव गतिस्त्वं गतिस्त्वं त्वमेका भवानि ॥१॥
भवाब्धावपारे महादुःखभीरुः पपात प्रकामी प्रलोभी प्रमत्तः ।
कुसंसारपाशप्रबद्धः सदाहं गतिस्त्वं गतिस्त्वं त्वमेका भवानि ॥२॥
न जानामि दानं न च ध्यानयोगं न जानामि तन्त्रं न च स्तोत्रमन्त्रम् ।
न जानामि पूजां न च न्यासयोगं गतिस्त्वं गतिस्त्वं त्वमेका भवानि ॥३॥
न जानामि पुण्यं न जानामि तीर्थं न जानामि मुक्तिं लयं वा कदाचित् ।
न जानामि भक्तिं व्रतं वापि मातर्- गतिस्त्वं गतिस्त्वं त्वमेका भवानि ॥४॥
कुकर्मी कुसङ्गी कुबुद्धिः कुदासः कुलाचारहीनः कदाचारलीनः ।
कुदृष्टिः कुवाक्यप्रबन्धः सदाहं गतिस्त्वं गतिस्त्वं त्वमेका भवानि ॥५॥
प्रजेशं रमेशं महेशं सुरेशं दिनेशं निशीथेश्वरं वा कदाचित् ।
न जानामि चान्यत् सदाहं शरण्ये गतिस्त्वं गतिस्त्वं त्वमेका भवानि ॥६॥
विवादे विषादे प्रमादे प्रवासे जले चानले पर्वते शत्रुमध्ये ।
अरण्ये शरण्ये सदा मां प्रपाहि गतिस्त्वं गतिस्त्वं त्वमेका भवानि ॥७॥
अनाथो दरिद्रो जरारोगयुक्तो महाक्षीणदीनः सदा जाड्यवक्त्रः ।
विपत्तौ प्रविष्टः प्रनष्टः सदाहं गतिस्त्वं गतिस्त्वं त्वमेका भवानि ॥८॥

इति श्रीमदादिशङ्कराचार्यविरचितं भवान्यष्टकं सम्पूर्णम्

Dedicated to

Late Shri Jagdish Prasad Kuriyal
Late Shri Acharya Gurudev Ramesh Chandra Sastri

Special Thanks to

Shri Mahadev Prasad Kuriyal
Shri Mati Krishna Devi
Shri Kavindra Istwal
Shri Nripesh Tiwari

Contents

Introduction

A Taste of Something More

There are moments when the world quiets, not from silence, but from a deeper presence. A breeze touches your skin and feels like a message. A song you have heard a hundred times suddenly moves you to tears. A single bite of food halts your thoughts, anchoring you to the now. These moments do not need explanation—they *feel* like something more.

We call them mystical, transcendent, or awakening. But they are, in truth, profoundly human. And they all begin in the same place: the senses.

We often think of spirituality as something above or beyond the body—a climb out of flesh, instinct, or emotion. But what if the path to the soul is not away from the senses, but *through* them? What if the body is not an obstacle to awakening, but its most faithful companion?

This book is a journey into the sensory world, serving as a spiritual map—a blend of psychology, spirituality, human behaviour, and physiology. Here, the five senses are not distractions, but sacred instruments. Each chapter explores how seeing, hearing, touching, tasting, and smelling are not only physical processes but deeply emotional and spiritual ones. We will explore how perception shapes reality, how the nervous system reflects our inner state, and how ancient wisdom and modern studies both point to the same truth: the body knows the way.

When we understand how our senses shape our thoughts, feelings, and states of awareness, we begin to see that enlightenment is not an escape from the world—it is an immersion into it: into this moment, this breath, this heartbeat.

A Taste of Enlightenment is not about abandoning the self. It is about coming home to it, fully—body, mind, and spirit.

- Chapter 1: The Soul within the Body

This chapter explores the perspectives of ancient traditions and modern science on the soul, introducing the concept that the human body is not separate from the spirit, but rather a vessel and translator of it. It discusses the spiritual significance of the nervous and endocrine systems in clear and accessible language.

- Chapter 2: The Language of the Senses

This chapter dives deep into the five physical senses—touch, taste, smell, sight, and sound—as well as the often-overlooked sixth sense: intuition. It describes how each sense shapes our reality and how sensory experience is a direct bridge to spiritual perception.

- Chapter 3: Touch – The Sacred Skin

This chapter examines the skin as the first organ of communication. Describes how touch affects emotional well-being, oxytocin release, and connection to others. It also delves into how healing practices, such as Reiki, massage, or simply being present, awaken deeper states of consciousness.

- Chapter 4: Sound – Vibrations of the Soul

It covers how sound impacts the nervous system and endocrine responses. Talks about music, chanting, and silence as sacred tools. It also includes scientific data on brainwave changes and spiritual practices, such as mantra meditation.

- Chapter 5: Sight – Seeing Beyond the Visible

It focuses on visual stimuli, the pineal gland (sometimes referred to as the "seat of the soul"), and symbolic vision, discussing how light, imagery, colours, and spiritual visions stimulate physiological and emotional transformation.

- Chapter 6: Smell – The Memory of Spirit

It explains how scent is linked to the limbic system and emotional memory, covering aromatherapy, sacred rituals, and how smells can awaken subconscious spiritual memories.

- Chapter 7: Taste – The Flavour of Awareness

It explores how food, fasting, mindful eating, and rituals like communion connect us to a higher self, incorporating the biology of taste and its connection to emotional and spiritual well-being.

- Chapter 8: Intuition – The Sixth Sense

It unpacks gut feelings, hunches, and dreams as messages from beyond the conscious mind. It also includes psychological theories of intuition and spiritual interpretations from mystics and modern thinkers alike.

- Chapter 9: Hormones – The Alchemy Within

It focuses on the endocrine system, exploring how hormones influence emotions, instincts, and higher awareness. It also discusses cortisol, dopamine, serotonin, oxytocin, and melatonin in the context of spiritual growth and personal experiences.

- Chapter 10: The Mind-Body-Spirit Continuum

It demonstrates how psychological processes, such as trauma, joy, and love, manifest in the body and impact the soul. It also introduces concepts like somatic memory, neuroplasticity, and emotional intelligence through a spiritual lens.

- Chapter 11: Breath – The Invisible Guide

It explains how breathing patterns regulate the nervous system, balance hormones, and foster inner peace. It also describes pranayama, breathwork, and spontaneous breathing in the context of mystical experiences.

- Chapter 12: Silence, Stillness, and the Inner Sense

It discusses the value of sensory withdrawal, meditation, and solitude, utilising ancient philosophies and current neuroscience to demonstrate how silence enhances spiritual clarity.

- Chapter 13: When the Body Becomes the Prayer

It brings together all the senses in everyday sacredness, discussing mindful living, embodiment, and honouring the body as a spiritual instrument.

- Chapter 14: The Science of Transcendence

It highlights research studies, experiments, and cross-cultural philosophies that validate spiritual experiences. Besides that, it also connects neuroscience, psychology, and physiology with mystical states of consciousness.

- Chapter 15: Reclaiming the Sacred in a Sensory World

This chapter calls to integrate all that we have learned into our daily lives, encouraging readers to see spiritual opportunities in every sensation and moment.

Chapter 1

The Soul within the Body

Section 1: The Silent Companion

From the very first moment of life, when a tiny heartbeat echoes within the womb, there is more than just flesh coming alive. There is a presence, quiet and ancient, that stirs in the spaces between each breath. We often refer to it as the soul. Though unseen and untouched, it pulses through the veins of our being, like an eternal whisper moving through our muscles, our emotions, and our thoughts. While the body grows and changes, the soul watches silently, like a companion who never leaves, even when we forget it is there.

In every culture across the world, people have searched for the soul—its location, its meaning, its purpose. Some believe it lives in the heart, where feelings bloom. Others believe it dwells in the brain, the place of consciousness. Some ancient texts describe it as residing in the breath, moving in and out with life itself. And others say it is not within the body at all, but beyond it, a field of energy that chooses the body as a temporary home. Whatever name or place we give it, the soul has always been considered the most profound truth of who we are.

Modern science may hesitate to speak of the soul, but it often finds itself brushing up against its mystery. Neurologists study the mind, trying to understand consciousness. Psychologists dive into emotion, trauma, memory, and identity. Endocrinologists map out the flow of hormones that shape our moods, desires, and instincts. And yet, when asked where the sense of self truly comes from—what it is that gives us awareness, meaning, or a longing to love—there are no definitive answers. The soul remains like a perfume in the air. You cannot catch it, but you know it is there.

Section 2: The Architecture of Being

The body is often seen as a machine—a collection of systems and cells, organs and blood, bones and breath. But when we look closely, we begin to see that this so-called machine is far more than biology. It responds to our moods, reflects our emotions, and even changes shape depending on how we live, what we feel, and what we believe. When someone is in love, their eyes shine brighter. When someone grieves, the body bends, the shoulders drop, and even the heartbeat slows. When someone is at peace, their breath is calm and steady, and their very presence seems to radiate warmth. The body is not just a container. It is a living mirror of our inner world.

Every cell in the body is like a small being, constantly listening and reacting to signals. These signals come from the brain, from hormones, from the nervous system, and—perhaps—from something more subtle. Scientific instruments may not yet detect the soul, but what if the soul is what brings unity to this orchestra? What if it is the conductor, silent yet essential, guiding the melody of our lives?

In ancient Eastern traditions, such as Ayurveda and Traditional Chinese Medicine, the body is seen as an extension of the soul. Illness is not only a physical imbalance—it is a spiritual misalignment. When someone becomes disconnected from their deeper self, the body suffers. On the eastern side, we are slowly beginning to recognise this as well. Psychosomatic medicine shows how thoughts and emotions can cause real symptoms. Stress can lead to high blood pressure, trauma can be stored in the muscles, and joy can strengthen the immune system. All of this suggests that the body is not separate from the soul, but its echo.

Section 3: The Nervous System – A Highway of Awareness

The human nervous system is a network of unimaginable complexity, stretching from the brain and spinal cord to every fingertip, every toe, and every organ. Like an intricate web, it carries messages that enable us to feel, move, remember, and imagine. But beyond its mechanical functions, the nervous system also holds something more mysterious—it is our bridge to awareness.

When we experience a spiritual moment—a sudden stillness in the forest, the feeling of unity during meditation, or a tearful release during prayer—those sensations pass through the nervous system. The heart rate slows, the pupils dilate, and the skin becomes sensitive. The body responds as if receiving a message from another world. We feel these moments not just in our minds, but throughout our entire being. This is because the nervous system is tuned to more than just survival; it is also tuned to meaning.

The vagus nerve, for example, is a significant and vital nerve that travels from the brain down through the chest and into the gut, controlling digestion, heart rate, and even aspects of voice and expression. But it is also involved in the body's response to love, empathy, and compassion. When we feel safe, seen, or spiritually open, the vagus nerve becomes active, allowing the body to relax and the mind to connect. It is as if the soul whispers through this pathway, telling the body, "You are home."

Section 4: The Heart as a Spiritual Organ

Though we often think of the brain as the command centre of the body, it is the heart that ancient traditions have honoured as the seat of the soul. Long before there were machines to measure brainwaves, people believed the heart held our wisdom, our love, and our inner truth. Even today, we speak in the language of the heart: heartache, heartfelt, broken-hearted, open-hearted, and whole-hearted. These words are not accidental. They point to a deeper reality, one that modern science is only beginning to explore.

Physiologically, the heart is more than a pump. It has its nervous system, sometimes referred to as the "heart brain." This system allows the heart to send signals to the brain and the rest of the body, influencing how we think, feel, and react. When the heart is calm, the brain becomes clearer. Conversely, when the heart is racing due to anxiety or fear, the brain struggles to focus. The two are in constant dialogue, creating a rhythm between thought and emotion.

Research conducted by institutions like the Heart-Math Institute shows that the heart generates an electromagnetic field that extends several feet outside the body. This field responds to our emotions, becoming erratic when we are angry or afraid, and harmonious when we are loving, compassionate, or grateful. Some researchers believe this field may even influence others around us. It is as though the soul communicates through this invisible language of the heart, radiating peace or pain into the space beyond our skin.

Spiritual practices across cultures—from Sufi whirling to Christian prayer, from Buddhist loving-kindness meditations to indigenous rituals—often involve focusing on the heart, not just as a physical muscle, but as a gateway, a door through which the soul breathes and blesses the world.

Section 5: Hormones and the Language of Feeling

The endocrine system is a hidden river that runs through us. It is made of glands that release hormones—chemical messengers that travel through the blood and shape our emotions, instincts, and even spiritual experiences. Though invisible to the eye, these messengers have profound effects. They tell us when to feel pleasure, when to rest, when to fear, and when to love.

Oxytocin, often referred to as the "bonding hormone," surges in moments of touch, affection, and trust. It is released during childbirth, breastfeeding, and orgasm. But it also rises during prayer, chanting, and shared sacred experiences. This hormone softens the boundaries between self and other, making us feel connected, safe, and open. In spiritual language, oxytocin allows us to taste oneness.

Then there is cortisol, the stress hormone. When we are anxious or under threat, cortisol floods the body, preparing us for danger. It raises blood pressure, sharpens alertness, and pulls us out of the present moment. In this state, it is difficult to meditate and feel a sense of grace or connection. Chronic stress becomes a wall between the body and the soul. That is why many spiritual practices, such as yoga, deep breathing, and mindfulness, are designed to help lower cortisol levels. They clear the path for inner stillness.

Dopamine and serotonin, two other key hormones, are tied to reward, happiness, and motivation. But they also rise during spiritual practices. When someone enters a deep state of meditation or loses themselves in devotion or dance, dopamine may be involved. These experiences are not just chemical; they are a combination of chemical and divine. The body responds to the soul's call with its sacred chemistry.

Section 6: The Body as a Temple

Throughout human history, various cultures have described the body as a temple—a sacred dwelling for the soul. This is not merely poetic language; it is a profound spiritual truth. The body is where spirit meets flesh, where breath becomes prayer, movement becomes ritual, and sensation becomes awareness. Every part of the body holds the potential for awakening.

The spine, for instance, is seen in yogic traditions as the central channel of energy. Along this channel lie the chakras—subtle centres of power and consciousness. These are not just metaphysical ideas. They correspond to principal nerve bundles and endocrine glands. The throat chakra is linked to the thyroid gland, the heart chakra rests near the thymus, and the solar plexus chakra is located near the adrenal glands. These locations are not accidental. They reflect a hidden unity between ancient wisdom and modern science.

Caring for the body, then, becomes a spiritual act. To eat mindfully, to sleep deeply, to move with grace—these are not just health choices. They are gestures of respect for the soul's home. Illness, in this view, is not a punishment; it is a message, a whisper from the soul asking for attention, rest, forgiveness, or change.

When we honour the body, we honour the soul. We allow it to move more freely, to speak more clearly, to guide us without resistance. We become vessels of something higher, not by escaping the body, but by living fully within it.

Section 7: The Breath That Carries Spirit

From the moment we are born to the instant we leave this world, one thing remains with us: breath. It is the quiet rhythm behind every experience, rising and falling like the ebb and flow of the ocean tide. We rarely notice it, yet it never leaves our side. In nearly every language, the word for breath is deeply linked to the word for soul or spirit. In Sanskrit, *prana* means both life force and breath. In Hebrew, *ruach* means both spirit and wind. In Greek, *pneuma* carries the same dual meaning. These are not coincidences—they are echoes of an ancient truth: the breath is the bridge between body and soul.

Scientifically, breathing is controlled by both conscious and unconscious systems. We can choose to hold it, slow it, or deepen it, but it also occurs naturally. This dual nature mirrors the soul itself—something we can touch in stillness, but which also flows quietly without our command. When we breathe deeply, primarily through the nose and into the belly, we activate the parasympathetic nervous system, shifting us into a state of calm, rest, and restoration. It is in this state that we feel peace, clarity, and connection.

Breathwork practices across cultures—from yogic pranayama to Tibetan Tummo, from Sufi breathing chants to Christian contemplative prayer—have long used the breath to enter higher states of awareness. Modern research shows that these practices can reduce stress hormones, regulate heart rate, and even alter brain wave patterns. Furthermore, they enable us to quiet the noise of the world and hear the voice of the soul. The breath is not just a function. It is a spiritual messenger, a sacred thread that ties together the physical and the divine.

Section 8: Memory in the Muscles, Emotion in the Bones

The body does not forget. Long after the mind has moved on, the body still carries echoes of past experiences. A scent, a sound, or a touch can bring back memories we thought were gone. This is because emotion is not just stored in the brain—it lives in the tissues, in the muscles, in the very way we stand and move. Trauma, for example, can create tightness in the chest, a shallow pattern of breathing, or guarding in the hips and shoulders. Joy, on the other hand, opens the body, makes us stand taller, breathe easier, and move more freely.

This concept, often referred to as *somatic memory*, is supported by modern psychology and body-centred therapies. Practices like somatic experiencing, EMDR, and trauma-informed yoga help people release emotional pain held in the body. However, ancient wisdom also recognised this. Indigenous cultures often use dance, movement, and song to heal. Shaking, crying, and even trembling are seen not as symptoms, but as sacred releases.

The soul, in this sense, lives not only in the heart or the mind, but in the flesh. Every scar, every stretch mark, every wrinkle is part of the soul's story. The body is a journal written in skin and sinew. And when we begin to listen to it—not just treat it, fix it, or judge it—we begin to understand the soul's quiet messages. Healing the body becomes an act of spiritual listening. Movement becomes meditation. Stillness becomes a homecoming.

Section 9: The Gut and the Second Brain

Deep within the belly lies a complex system of nerves, often referred to as the enteric nervous system, also known as the "second brain." This network contains more neurons than the spinal cord and is capable of sensing, feeling, and responding. It governs digestion but also plays a crucial role in mood, immunity, and emotional balance. Scientists now know that over 90% of the body's serotonin—a key hormone in happiness and well-being—is produced in the gut. The gut and the brain are in constant communication, connected by the vagus nerve in an unbroken loop of influence.

However, beyond its biological functions, the gut is also deeply symbolic. We speak of "gut feelings," "butterflies in the stomach," or "sinking feelings." These are not just expressions. They point to a deep awareness held in the core of our being. The gut is where many of us first feel fear. It tightens when we are anxious, churns when something is wrong, and softens when we feel safe. This intuitive intelligence is often faster than the thought process. Some spiritual traditions believe the belly is the seat of instinct, the place where the soul's wisdom first arises before the mind translates it.

When we learn to listen to the gut—not just its hunger, but its guidance—we reconnect with a primal form of knowing. Meditation, deep breathing, and dietary care can all help restore harmony here. But so can silence, honesty, and trust. When we create inner safety, the belly relaxes. When the belly relaxes, the soul speaks.

Section 10: Whispers of the Soul in Daily Life

It is easy to imagine the soul as something distant, something only touched in moments of silence or stillness. However, the truth is that the soul is always present. It speaks in the small, quiet ways: in the chill that rises on the skin during a song, in the way our body leans toward someone we trust, in the feeling of tears rising for no reason at all. These are not just emotions or reactions. They are the soul's language, written in sensation.

The body is constantly translating the soul into motion, into posture, into feeling. A smile that comes before thought, a tear that falls before understanding—these are the signs. And when we start to notice them, when we honour them, we begin to live in deeper alignment. We realize that the soul is not something we have to chase or create. It is already here. It is woven into the fabric of our being

To live spiritually does not mean to escape the body. It means to return to it fully, to listen with reverence, to treat it not as a burden but as a sacred vessel. It means to walk, breathe, eat, and rest as if every action is a prayer because it is.

Section 11: The Body in Sacred Traditions

Across the world's great spiritual traditions, the body is often honoured in symbolic and ritualistic ways. In Hinduism, the body is seen as the vehicle of *dharma*, a sacred duty to live rightly. Yogic practices were never meant to make the body perfect in appearance; they were meant to prepare it for stillness, to make it a steady base through which the soul could shine. In Christianity, the idea that the body is the "temple of the Holy Spirit" speaks to this reverence. In Islam, cleanliness of the body is seen as a form of devotion, and prayer involves full-body gestures, such as bowing, kneeling, and touching the earth. Judaism teaches that the body is a creation of God and should be treated with dignity. In Buddhism, the breath, posture, and even the way one walks are integral to the path to awakening.

Even indigenous traditions, which have long been misunderstood or dismissed by Western systems, carry this wisdom deeply. The body is painted, danced, and sung through. Illness is seen not just as a physical disruption but as a spiritual imbalance, and healing involves realigning the body with the rhythms of nature and the soul. These traditions do not separate matter and spirit. They see them as one, as different waves of the same ocean.

Modern life often pulls us away from this sacred view. We are taught to compare our bodies, to judge them, to fix them. We are taught to live in our heads, chasing thoughts, neglecting breath, ignoring pain. But the wisdom of the body is not lost—it only waits for our return. It waits for us to treat it as the spiritual partner that it is, not just a shell but a song.

Section 12: Science and the Soul – A Widening Bridge

For many years, science and spirituality stood on opposite shores, unwilling to speak to each other. One dealt in measurement, the other in mystery. But slowly, steadily, a bridge is forming. Neuroscientists are now studying the effects of meditation on the brain and finding increased grey matter in areas linked to compassion and self-awareness. Psychologists are exploring how trauma reshapes the body's responses and how healing can occur not just through words, but through movement, touch, and breath.

Endocrinologists are examining how hormones influence not only behaviour but also transcendence. For example, melatonin, a hormone associated with sleep and the circadian rhythm, also plays a role in mystical experiences. The pineal gland, which secretes melatonin, has long been referred to as the "third eye" in many traditions. Although we may not have a full scientific explanation for the soul, we are beginning to understand the systems through which it operates.

Research into near-death experiences, spontaneous healing, and moments of profound insight during meditation or prayer is opening new doors. It suggests that consciousness may not be limited to the brain, and that there may be layers to our awareness—some biological, some beyond.

Rather than threatening spirituality, science is beginning to support it, not by replacing it, but by honouring the mystery it points toward. The body, when studied deeply, becomes a map of the sacred. Every organ, every nerve, every molecule becomes part of the unfolding story of the soul.

Section 13: The Integration of Body and Soul

We are not spirits trapped in bodies. We are spirits expressed through bodies. The two are not enemies—they are lovers. The body is the canvas, and the soul is the artist. Each movement, each breath, each heartbeat is a stroke of divine intention. When we recognise this, we stop fighting the body. We begin to live within it with care and kindness.

Spirituality is not about escaping the world. It is about becoming fully alive in it. It is about tasting, touching, and sensing with depth and presence. It is about using the senses not just for pleasure but for awakening. When we walk barefoot on the earth, feel the sun on our skin, or close our eyes in stillness, we are not stepping away from spirituality—we are stepping into it.

To integrate the body and soul is to become whole. It is to realise that enlightenment does not happen above the head but within the chest, the belly, the breath. It is to understand that wisdom is not only read—it is felt, lived, and carried in the way we sit, speak, and sleep.

We begin to ask different questions: What does my soul feel in my chest today? What is my breath telling me? Where is my body holding sadness or joy? These questions do not demand answers—they invite a relationship—a sacred intimacy between the self and the soul.

Section 14: A Living Temple, a Walking Prayer

When we see the body as sacred, our life becomes a prayer. The way we eat becomes a form of communion. The way we move becomes a kind of dance. The way we rest becomes an offering. We begin to trust the sensations we feel, rather than fearing them. We begin to listen more and fix less. We begin to open to the idea that the soul is not a separate light, but the light moving through every cell.

This view does not require belief in any particular religion. It asks only that we be present, that we slow down, that we feel, and that we allow our bodies to guide us toward what feels true, kind, and whole.

And when we live this way—present to the body, open to the soul—we find that life itself becomes spiritual, not in rare moments, but in every breath. The soul no longer feels distant; it feels near, like the warmth in our hands, the wind on our face, the stillness behind our eyes.

This is the taste of enlightenment. Not a distant peak to be climbed, but a presence to be lived, right here in the body, right now, in this breath.

Chapter 2

The Language of the Senses

Section 1: Touch – The Sacred Skin

From the moment a baby enters the world, even before it can see clearly or hear with understanding, it knows the language of touch. The warmth of a mother's chest, the gentle pressure of being cradled, the rhythmic beating of another human heart against its tiny frame—all of these say: You are here. You are safe. You are loved. Long before we can form words, touch teaches us about connection, belonging, and care.

The skin is the largest organ in the human body, serving as our outermost layer and the boundary between the world within and the world around us. However, it is more than a boundary; it is a vast field of sensation, a delicate map filled with thousands of nerve endings that respond to pressure, temperature, pain, and pleasure. It holds the power to awaken memories, soothe anxiety, and communicate without speech. When someone holds our hand, it can say more than a thousand words. When someone brushes against us gently, it can stir feelings we did not know were buried. Touch is not only physical—it is emotional, psychological, and spiritual.

Scientific research continues to reveal the importance of this sense. Studies show that babies who are not touched enough in their early days can suffer developmental delays. They may grow, but they often struggle emotionally, as their nervous systems lack the comforting feedback that touch provides. In contrast, babies who are held, rocked, and touched with care tend to grow more resilient and emotionally balanced. The body, from the beginning, is programmed to thrive on safe, nurturing contact.

As we grow older, this need does not vanish—it only becomes more hidden. In many societies, especially those that value independence and emotional restraint, the human need for touch is often neglected. Adults may go days or even weeks without experiencing meaningful physical contact. However, the need remains. When we are hugged, when someone touches our shoulder during a time of grief, or when we sit close to someone we trust, our bodies recall something ancient. The heart rate slows, stress hormones drop, and oxytocin—the hormone of bonding and trust—rises. The body relaxes not just into physical comfort, but into a more profound sense of belonging.

From a spiritual perspective, touch opens a doorway into the present moment. It brings our awareness out of the cluttered mind and into the body. In mindfulness practices, simple activities like feeling the ground beneath the feet or placing a hand over the heart are used to anchor attention. They are not just techniques—they are rituals that remind us of the sacredness of embodiment. In these moments, the body becomes not a distraction from spirit, but the very path toward it. In religious and healing traditions across the world, touch holds a central place. In Christianity, the laying on of hands is a symbol of healing and grace. In *Reiki*, a Japanese practice, the practitioner channels energy through the hands to bring balance to the recipient. In *Ayurveda*, warm oil is used in massage to calm the nervous system and align the subtle energies of the body. *Shamans* in South America may use their hands to draw sickness out of the body in ceremonial healing. Even in the simple act of a child falling and being kissed on the forehead, there is power—because love travels through touch.

Touch also teaches boundaries. Just as safe and nurturing contact can help us feel whole, harmful or invasive touch can cause deep wounds. Trauma that enters through the skin leaves marks that are not always visible, but they are real. The body may flinch at future touches, even loving ones. The nervous system learns to fear, to brace, to close. Healing from such wounds often involves relearning the language of safe touch. Therapy, somatic practices, and gentle reintroduction to comfort can help the body unlearn its fear and rediscover trust.

This is why body-based healing is so essential. Talk therapy alone may not reach the layers of pain stored in the muscles, the fascia, and the body's very breath patterns. Practices such as yoga, craniosacral therapy, and dance therapy offer ways to reconnect with the self, not just mentally, but also physically. When we allow our body to move freely, to be held, or to rest in stillness, the soul finds space to rise again. There is also the profound experience of spiritual ecstasy that comes through touch. In some traditions, mystics have described feeling divine presence as a sensation on the skin—a breeze, a tingling, a warmth. These are not hallucinations, but embodied encounters with something greater. The soul, it seems, speaks through sensation. The body, far from being an obstacle to spirituality, becomes its translator.

Touch is also profoundly connected to intimacy. Sexuality, when approached with reverence, becomes a sacred exchange of energy. In *tantric* traditions, the act of physical union is not simply about pleasure—it is a pathway to the divine. The merging of bodies is seen as a symbol of the soul's longing for unity. When entered with presence and respect, the act of touching another can become a meditation, a prayer, a communion beyond words. In daily life, we can reconnect with this sacred relationship through touch. We can pause to feel the sunlight on our skin, offering hugs with presence, not just habit. We can place our hands over our hearts when we feel lost, whispering inwardly, "I am here." We can wash our bodies not with rush or shame, but with gratitude. We can let our feet rest on the grass or sand and feel the earth supporting us. These are small rituals, but they are doorways to something greater.

In a world filled with distractions, noise, and disconnection, touch brings us home—home to our bodies, home to one another, and home to the soul that lives in sensation. When we understand this, touch is no longer just a sense—it is a spiritual practice. It is a language that does not lie. It says: I see you. I feel you. I am with you. And in this presence, something divine awakens.

Section 2: Sound – Vibrations of the Soul

Long before humans spoke words, they made sounds. The hum of a mother soothing her baby, the chant of the first dawn prayer, the cry that echoes through the trees when danger is near—these ancient vibrations are woven into the roots of our existence. Sound is not just communication; it is present energy in motion. It reaches into the body not through logic, but through resonance. It bypasses the mind and goes directly to the heart, the nerves, the cells. When we hear a song that stirs tears in our eyes or a voice that makes us feel safe, something within us responds without needing to understand. That something is the soul.

The sense of hearing is often underestimated, yet it profoundly shapes our experience of the world. It begins in the womb. Around the fifth month of pregnancy, the fetus begins to hear. The mother's heartbeat, the murmur of her voice, the rhythm of her footsteps—all are absorbed into the growing consciousness. This first connection with sound is deeply emotional, creating the foundation for how we later respond to tone, music, silence, and speech.

Our ears never fully close. Even in deep sleep, the auditory system remains partly alert. It is as though some part of us is always listening—always ready to receive, respond, or awaken. In meditation traditions, the practice of deep listening is not just about hearing external sounds, but about turning inward to hear the subtle music of the self. What do we hear when the world goes quiet? What arises in the stillness between breaths?

In spiritual practice, sound has always held a sacred place. Chanting, for instance, is found in almost every religious path. The repetition of syllables, prayers, or divine names is more than tradition—it is a form of vibration therapy for the soul. In Hinduism and Buddhism, mantras such as *Om*, *So Hum*, or *Om Mani Padme Hum* are believed to align the body and mind with universal frequencies. In Christianity, Gregorian chants fill cathedrals with waves of reverence that seem to lift the spirit upward. In Sufism, the whirling dervishes chant *La ilaha illallah*, not just with their mouths, but with their entire being, spinning into the silence of the Divine.

Modern science has begun to catch up with these ancient insights. Neuroscientists now understand that music can alter brainwave patterns. Slow, rhythmic music can induce alpha states in the brain, associated with calmness, openness, and creativity. Specific frequencies are even used in therapy. Binaural beats, which play slightly different frequencies in each ear, are used to guide the brain into meditative states. These are not just theories—they are experiences. When we listen to a piece of music that moves us, or to the ocean's steady breath, something in us shifts. We are brought into alignment.

There is also a biological reason why sound can evoke a spiritual feeling. The bones in our ears vibrate with each sound wave, and the vagus nerve, which is linked to the parasympathetic nervous system, connects through the inner ear. When we hear something soothing, this nerve is stimulated, activating the body's relaxation response. Our breathing slows, our muscles release tension, and our mind quiets. This is why the sound of chanting, or the resonance of a singing bowl, can feel like it is entering not just the ears, but the soul itself. Silence, too, is a kind of sound, or rather, a space where sound can be fully felt. In silence, we hear more than just the absence of noise—we begin to hear the deeper layers of ourselves, our fears, our hopes, our rawness, our longing. Many spiritual paths emphasise silence as a doorway to the Divine. Not because silence is empty, but because it is full. It is the canvas upon which the soul paints its softest colours.

Sacred sound is also found in nature. The rustle of wind in leaves, the crackling of fire, the sound of rain on a roof, birdsong at dawn—these are the original hymns of the earth. They require no interpretation, yet they bring peace, perspective, and sometimes a sense of the eternal. To stand in a forest and listen is to enter a cathedral not built by hands. In healing, sound is increasingly being used to treat anxiety, trauma, and emotional wounds. Sound baths, where gongs, bowls, and chimes wash over the body in waves of vibration, are known to reduce stress and increase clarity. Voice therapy, where the individual is encouraged to use their voice to release stored tension or emotion, taps into the body's capacity to heal itself through resonance.

Sound is also memory. A song can transport us instantly to another time, another feeling. A few notes can bring back a love, a heartbreak, or a moment of awe. These memories are not just mental—they are physical. The body remembers, and the soul remembers. That is why we cry when we hear a song we have not heard in years. It opens a door.

In daily life, we can begin to reclaim the sacredness of sound. We can choose the music we listen to not just based on preference, but based on energy. We can create moments of silence to listen within. We can chant or hum during moments of stress. We can speak with greater intention, knowing that our words carry vibrations that affect not only others but also ourselves. Our voice can become a tool of healing, our ears an opening to wonder.

The soul listens. It is always listening, not just to what is said, but how it is said, not just to external noise, but to the deeper rhythm beneath it all. In the end, sound is not just something we hear—it is something we become: a vibration of consciousness, echoing across time, reminding us that we are not separate; we are part of the song.

Section 3: Sight–Seeing Beyond the Visible

Of all the senses, sight is perhaps the most dominant in the modern world. Images surround us, flooded with colours and screens, bombarded by symbols and signs. Our eyes are constantly processing, constantly scanning, trying to make sense of everything we see. Yet, despite all this visual input, most of us rarely stop to consider what it means to see, not just in the physical sense, but in the emotional, psychological, and spiritual sense. What does it truly mean to see?

The eyes are miraculous organs. Each eye contains over 100 million photoreceptors, tiny cells that convert light into electrical signals. These signals travel through the optic nerve into the brain, where they are interpreted as colour, shape, movement, and form. We see because our brains turn photons into meaning. Yet we see not only with our eyes—we see with our memory, our culture, our emotions, our beliefs. Two people can look at the same sunset and have entirely different experiences. One may feel awe and joy, while another may feel nostalgia or sadness. What we see is shaped by who we are.

From a physiological standpoint, sight is an incredibly complex process. Light enters the eye, is focused by the lens, hits the retina, and is translated by the brain into a coherent image. However, the miracle goes even further. The brain not only just registers what the eye captures—it selects, organises, and fills in missing pieces. The image we see is as much constructed as it is received. The eye takes in only a small part of the world; the brain fills in the rest, based on patterns, memory, and expectation. We see what we expect to see, and we see what we believe is there.

This has powerful implications. If we believe the world is hostile, we are more likely to notice danger. If we believe the world is beautiful, we are more likely to notice wonder. Our inner state shapes our perception. In this way, vision becomes a mirror of the soul. When the heart is open, the world looks different. When the mind is quiet, colours seem deeper and textures seem richer. To heal the way we see, we must begin by healing the way we are within.

Spiritual traditions have long spoken of a deeper kind of seeing—one that transcends the physical eyes. In Christianity, this is referred to as "seeing with the eyes of the heart." In Buddhism, practitioners speak of the "Dharma eye"—the ability to see truth clearly. In Sufism, the "inner eye" or "eye of the soul" is the gateway to divine knowledge. Additionally, in Hindu and yogic philosophy, the "third eye," located at the centre of the forehead, is a symbol of higher perception and intuition.

This "third eye" is often associated with the pineal gland, a small gland in the centre of the brain that produces melatonin and helps regulate sleep cycles. Though science has not confirmed the pineal gland as a literal site of spiritual vision, many mystics and seekers report that when they enter deep states of meditation, they feel pressure or warmth in the area between the brows. Some describe inner visions, lights, or imagery that is not visible with the physical eyes. These experiences, while subjective, suggest that seeing is not confined to the outer world. The soul, too, has vision.

In psychology, we often use visual metaphors to describe insight, as in "I see what you mean," "It dawned on me," "A flash of understanding." These expressions reveal how deeply sight is tied to inner clarity. Dreams, imagination, and visualisation are also forms of vision—ones that occur entirely within. Athletes and performers often use visualisation to prepare for success, seeing in their minds what they want to create. Healers and shamans may use guided imagery to help people release trauma or call in strength. What we see inside becomes what we create outside.

However, sight can also deceive. We live in a culture that places enormous value on appearance. The pressure to look a certain way—to conform to visual ideals—can cause deep spiritual wounds. Many people feel disconnected from their worth because they believe their bodies do not meet specific standards. The mirror becomes an enemy, hiding the soul behind shame. To reclaim spiritual sight, we must begin to see ourselves not with the eyes of judgment, but with the eyes of compassion. The body is not something to be looked at; it is a sacred vessel, a living presence, and a miracle.

Beauty, in the spiritual sense, is not about symmetry or perfection. It is about presence. A face lined with age, a scar from childbirth, the tired eyes of someone who has survived grief—these too are beautiful because they carry the story of the soul. When we begin to see beauty in what is real, raw, and human, we begin to see with the eyes of love. And love is the soul's true vision.

Sight is also deeply linked to light. We only see because of light. Light bounces off objects and enters the eye, creating colour and form. In spiritual traditions, light is often a metaphor for truth, divinity, or awakening. To be "enlightened" means to be filled with light. To live in "darkness" means to be lost, confused, or disconnected. These metaphors remind us that seeing is more than a biological phenomenon—it is an existential experience. We are all seeking light, not just with our eyes, but with our souls.

Nature teaches us this beautifully. Observe how a plant turns toward the sun, bending and stretching in its quest for light. The soul does the same; it longs to turn toward what is good, what is true, and what is whole. And like the plant, it needs the right conditions to thrive—rest, nourishment, space, and light.

In everyday life, we can begin to practise spiritual sight. We can slow down and look at the faces around us—not just glance, but see. We can walk in nature and let our eyes rest on leaves, clouds, and the curve of water. We can look into a candle flame and see more than fire—we can see the quiet centre of our being. We can look into a mirror and soften our gaze, letting love replace critique. We can close our eyes and ask, "What does my soul want me to see today?"

Vision is not just what happens when our eyes are open. Vision is what we choose to focus on, what we choose to believe, and what we allow ourselves to notice. When we begin to see with presence, compassion, and wonder, we awaken to a more profound truth: the world is not just a matter; it has meaning. It is not just a surface; it is a soul.

To see clearly is not to see more; it is to see deeper, beneath appearances and illusion, into the sacredness of things and the sacredness of self. This is the gift of sight, not just as a sense, but as a way of being. When we receive it fully, the world becomes alive—each colour becomes a prayer, each shadow becomes an invitation, each glance becomes a doorway.

And in that moment, we realise that we are not just looking at the world, we are being looked at, too, by life, by love, by the quiet presence that lives behind all things. We are being seen, and we are being called to see truly.

Chapter 3

The Sacred Sense – Touch and the Soul

Section 1: Touch as the First Sense

Before we learn to see the world, before sound shapes meaning, even before breath fully finds rhythm, we begin by feeling. Touch is the first sense to develop in the womb. Long before an infant can open its eyes or respond to voices, the skin is already alive with the world, pressing, receiving, sensing. It is through touch that the embryo first understands: I am here. There is a space around me. There is motion. There is another.

In the fluid temple of the womb, the skin becomes the first veil through which the soul expresses itself. It is not merely a barrier; it is a portal, a medium. The flutter of amniotic fluid, the vibrations of the mother's heartbeat, the gentle stretching of developing limbs—these are the original hymns of sensation, the pre-verbal verses of existence. Here, even without language, the growing life begins to "know" through touch. This knowing is ancient, intuitive, and sacred.

Across all cultures, the first act of comfort is touch. A crying baby is not reasoned with—it is held. A grieving person is not advised—they are embraced. A fearful animal is soothed by touch, as are humans in their most vulnerable states. This universal instinct points to a profound truth: touch communicates beyond words, telling the nervous system, "You are safe" and reminding the soul, "You are not alone." In this way, touch becomes both presence and promise.

The earliest human societies understood this intuitively. Tribal and indigenous traditions across the globe have long incorporated touch into their healing rituals. Hands placed over wounds, gentle rubbing of oils on skin, shared dances where shoulders touch and bodies move in rhythm—these were not seen as superficial acts, but as medicine. Even now, the laying of hands in spiritual healing, the sacred anointing in temple rituals, and the symbolic gestures of *mudras* all reflect the timeless sanctity of touch.

From the moment of birth to the threshold of death, the human body remains exquisitely sensitive to the touch of another. In moments of ecstasy or agony, joy or sorrow, it is through touch that emotions become embodied. A caress can awaken deep love, a hand on the back can offer unspoken strength, and the gentle brushing of fingers can ignite memory, desire, and even a profound sense of awareness. The skin remembers.

Modern psychology and somatic therapy recognise this stored history of touch. Traumatic touch—abuse, harm, neglect—can remain embedded in the nervous system long after the event has passed. Conversely, healing touch—safe, consensual, loving—can release those buried patterns. It is not the intellect that heals these wounds; it is the body, the skin, and the touch. The nervous system speaks a different language, and it remembers far more than we think.

As we age, touch may become less frequent, but it is no less needed. Elderly individuals often experience touch deprivation, which can lead to loneliness and cognitive decline. Yet a simple hand massage, a gentle hug, or a shared moment of holding hands can restore connection and vitality. In this, the soul does not age; it still reaches out, still responds to warmth, presence, and pressure. The language of touch does not grow old—it grows deeper.

From the lover's gentle embrace to the child's tug at a sleeve, from the sacred placing of ash on the forehead to the cooling water poured during ritual ablution, touch transcends mere sensation. It is meaning made manifest, spirit expressed through skin.

In the next section, we will delve into the sacred texts of India to explore how the *Vedas, Upanishads,* and the *Bhagavad Gita* honour this most primal of senses, not just as a human experience, but as a divine expression.

Section 2: The Language of the Skin – Shlokas and Sacred Echoes

The ancient seers of India did not view the senses as distractions from the divine. They saw them as sacred channels—pathways through which the soul could interact with the manifest world and also return to its source. Among the senses, **touch** held a place of deep reverence, woven through hymns, meditations, and philosophical insights across the *Vedas, Upanishads,* and the *Bhagavad Gita.*

To understand how the Vedic mind approached the sense of touch, one must first look not at science, but at *experience.* In Vedic thought, experience is the highest authority. The *ṛṣis*—the seers who composed the *Vedas*—did not speculate; they realised. They sat in stillness, became one with the rhythms of breath and being, and listened deeply to what the body and cosmos revealed. And in this stillness, they discovered that the skin was not just a sheath of flesh—it was a veil between the seen and the unseen.

The Taittiriya Upanishad and the Touch of Ananda

In the *Taittiriya Upanishad,* we find a profound map of the self, what is known as the ***pañca-kośa***, or the five sheaths of being. These sheaths progress from the gross physical to the subtle spiritual: *Annamaya Kośa* – the sheath of food (the physical body), *Prāṇamaya Kośa* – the sheath of energy (breath and vital forces), *Manomaya Kośa* – the sheath of mind (thoughts and emotions), *Vijñānamaya Kośa* – the sheath of wisdom (intellect and discernment), and *Ānandamaya Kośa* – the sheath of bliss (the innermost soul layer).

The first sheath, Annamaya, is the most directly connected with the sense of touch. It is through the physical body that we first experience the world. But the *Upanishad* teaches us that *touch* is not limited to this outer layer—it moves inward. The *bliss* that radiates from the deepest layer of the soul is not just an abstract feeling; it is felt and experienced from within.

A powerful shloka from the *Taittiriya Upanishad* says:

"रसोवैसः। रसं ह्येवायं लब्ध्वा आनन्दी भवति।"

Raso vai saḥ. Rasaṁ hyevāyaṁ labdhvā ānandī bhavati.

(He is indeed rasa. Having obtained rasa, one becomes blissful.)

Here, ***rasa*** refers to the essence, taste, or even touch, which is the very felt sense of divine presence. The text suggests that when we *experience* this *rasa*, rather than just thinking about it, we become truly blissful. This is not an intellectual realisation. It is a sensory and spiritual one. And the skin, the body, becomes the very temple through which that rasa flows.

The Vedas and Sparśa (स्पर्श)

In the *Rigveda*, the word स्पर्श —meaning *touch*—appears in several hymns. One of the earliest uses is in describing the touch of Agni, the sacred fire.

"त्वं हि स्पर्शो अग्ने देवतानाम्"

Tvaṁ hi sparśo agne devatānām

(You, O Agni, are the touch of the gods.)

Agni is not merely fire. He is consciousness in radiant form. When the fire is touched—not just physically, but inwardly—there is a purification, a transformation. Here, touch is used to describe *communion.* The gods are not only seen or worshipped—they are *touched* through presence, through offering, through the fire.

In Vedic rituals, touch is essential. The water sprinkled during purification, the gesture of offering grains into fire, the clasping of hands in marriage—all are acts of sacred touch. The body is never excluded from worship. It is not a hindrance—it is a conduit.

Bhagavad Gita – Mastery over the Senses

In the *Bhagavad Gita,* Lord Krishna repeatedly refers to the mastery and understanding of the senses as the foundation for spiritual liberation. Among the senses, ***sparśa*** **(touch)** is highlighted as a source of both pleasure and bondage.

"ये हि संस्पर्शजा भोगाः दुःखयोनय एव ते।"

Ye hi saṁsparśajā bhogāḥ duḥkha-yonaya eva te

(The pleasures that arise from contact with the senses are wombs of suffering.)

— *Bhagavad Gita 5.22*

Here, Krishna speaks to Arjuna about the transient pleasure that arises from contact—the kind of touch driven by craving, grasping, or ignorance. He is not condemning the sense of touch itself. Instead, he is pointing to **attachment to the external**—a misuse of the sacred faculty of touch.

In another shloka, Krishna offers a more nuanced perspective:

"शीतोष्णसुखदुःखेषु समं सङ्गविवर्जितम्।"

Śītoṣṇa-sukha-duḥkheṣu samaṁ saṅga-vivarjitam

(One who remains balanced in cold and heat, pleasure and pain, and free from attachment...)

— *Bhagavad Gita 12.18*

Here, touch sensations like heat and cold are mentioned. The spiritual aspirant is not the one who escapes sensation, but the one who remains balanced within it. Sensation is not the enemy; rather, it is reaction. Krishna's teaching is not about numbing the body, but about transcending compulsive reaction.

Thus, in the *Gita,* touch becomes a teacher. Every sensation is a chance to witness. Every response is a mirror. And through this observation, the soul begins to awaken.

Interpreting Touch through Vedanta

Vedanta, the philosophical culmination of the *Vedas*, offers a profound understanding of the senses. The sense organs (*indriyas)* are described as part of the *antahkaraṇa*—the inner instrument through which consciousness interacts with the world. Touch is governed by the *tvak indriya* (skin organ), connected to the element of air (*vāyu*).

Why air? It is because touch requires subtlety. It is not seen or heard, but it moves, like wind, across the surface of the skin and into the deeper layers of awareness. Just as wind can stir still waters, touch stirs the soul. In Vedantic practice, this understanding is not just a theory—it is put into practice through meditation.

To sit and observe touch—the feel of the air on the skin, the contact of breath at the nostrils, the pressure of the ground beneath—is to enter a state of profound presence. In that presence, the ego begins to dissolve, and what remains is awareness itself.

Section 3: Neuroscience of Touch – The Sacred Pathway

Touch is not simply a physical encounter—it is a biological symphony that begins with sensation and culminates in consciousness. To touch is to be in direct conversation with the nervous system, and through that system, to engage with the deepest architecture of human experience. The ancient sages intuited this when they described touch as *sparśa*, a subtle communion between the outer world and the inner being. Today, modern neuroscience is beginning to reveal just how intricate and sacred that communion truly is.

The Skin: The First Gate

The journey of touch begins at the skin, the human body's largest and most sensitive organ. Stretching over two square meters and weighing several kilograms, the skin is more than just a protective covering; it is an intelligent interface, a sensory radar embedded with millions of receptors, each specialised to detect different kinds of information.

These receptors fall into several primary categories:

- **Meissner's corpuscles**, located near the skin's surface, are responsible for detecting light touch and changes in texture.
- **Merkel's discs**, also located near the skin's surface, provide information about pressure and shape.
- **Pacinian corpuscles**, located deeper in the skin, respond to vibration and rapid changes in pressure.
- **Ruffini endings**, even more sensitive, are responsive to skin stretch and sustained pressure.
- **Free nerve endings**, spread throughout, detect pain, temperature, and crude touch.

These sensory receptors are not scattered randomly; they are exquisitely concentrated in areas of high sensitivity, such as the fingertips, lips, face, and genitals. This distribution reflects the human need for both survival and intimacy. We use our fingers to feel tools and surfaces, our lips to kiss, speak, and connect, and our skin not just to touch but to *know.*

When you gently run your fingers along silk, or feel the warmth of the sun on your arm, or sense a soft breeze brushing your cheek, it is not your skin alone that feels; it is **you**, the whole self, participating in sensation. The receptors are merely the doorway. What enters through them travels a miraculous path.

The Ascending Pathway: From Skin to Brain

The moment a touch receptor is activated, it generates an electrical impulse. This impulse travels along afferent nerve fibres—essentially, sensory pathways carrying information from the body toward the brain. These fibres enter the spinal cord through the dorsal root ganglia, a cluster of nerves that acts like a central hub for incoming sensations.

From the spinal cord, touch signals take one of two primary pathways:

- The Dorsal Column-Medial Lemniscal Pathway is fast and precise. This pathway carries delicate touch, vibration, and proprioception (the sense of body position). It ascends directly to the medulla, crosses over to the opposite side, and continues to the thalamus, a key relay station.
- The Spinothalamic Tract, which is slower and carries crude sensations of touch, pain, and temperature, enters the spinal cord, crosses immediately to the opposite side, and then travels up to the thalamus.

The thalamus, located deep within the brain, acts as a central hub for sensory data. It filters and forwards information to various areas of the cerebral cortex, especially the somatosensory cortex in the parietal lobe, where touch is consciously felt.

In this moment, just milliseconds after the skin is touched, you become aware - "Something touched me." You know its pressure, its texture, its location. Your brain has built an internal map of your body, known as the homunculus, where each body part has a corresponding representation in the cortex. The lips and hands occupy much more space than the legs or back, not because they are larger, but because they are more sensitive and significant in our interaction with the world.

The Emotional Brain: Touch and Feeling

But the journey of touch does not end in the cortex. Touch also travels to the limbic system, the seat of emotion and memory. The amygdala, hippocampus, and hypothalamus all receive touch-related data, especially when that touch is meaningful, surprising, or associated with experience.

This is why a hug from a loved one feels different from the same pressure applied by a stranger. It is not just the sensation—it is the emotional signature attached to it. Touch has the power to awaken joy, calm, desire, longing, and even grief. It can rekindle old memories, open emotional wounds, or provide healing.

One of the most remarkable aspects of touch is its ability to trigger the release of oxytocin, often referred to as the "bonding hormone." Oxytocin promotes trust, reduces anxiety, and strengthens social bonds. It is released during affectionate touch, childbirth, breastfeeding, and even during acts of prayer or spiritual surrender. It literally softens the nervous system, making us more open, more connected, more whole.

Other hormones are also involved. Dopamine, the reward molecule, can surge in response to pleasurable touch. Endorphins, the body's natural painkillers, are released with massage or a gentle caress. Cortisol, the stress hormone, drops when we feel held or comforted. In this way, the body's chemistry is not just biological—it is spiritual. It responds to love, care, and presence, remembering safety and opening in trust.

The Mirror Within: Touch, Consciousness, and the Self

Recent research in neuroscience has introduced us to the concept of mirror neurons—brain cells that fire not only when we act, but also when we observe someone else performing the same action. These neurons may also respond when we see someone being touched. This means that even witnessing touch can activate our sensory systems, evoking empathy, compassion, or even physical sensation.

This mirroring may be part of how spiritual connection is born. When we witness someone in deep prayer or see a ritual performed with devotion, we feel something stir in ourselves. It is not a belief—it is a felt resonance. We are touched without being touched, and our nervous system recognises this as genuine.

Touch, in this sense, becomes not only a sense but a form of awareness. It reminds us that we are embodied beings, existing in space and time and that we are not only minds floating above the world, but souls grounded within the sacred geography of the body. The nervous system is not a cold network of wires—it is a divine web, woven by evolution and spirit, designed to experience both pain and ecstasy, separation and union.

Section 4: Touch as Philosophy – Duality, Unity, and the Soul

Touch is a paradox. It is the sense that proves separation—"I feel this, so it is not me"—and at the same time, it is the sense that dissolves boundaries—"I feel this, therefore I belong to it." In this paradox lies one of the greatest spiritual truths: duality is not the end, but the beginning of unity. From the Vedantic vision of *Advaita* (non-dualism) to the poetic mysticism of *Tantra,* to the psycho-spiritual revelations of modern psychology, touch has always been far more than contact between surfaces. It is an encounter between realities.

The Duality of Touch

Touch affirms distinctions like I am not the air I feel, I am not the flame that warms me, I am not the stone beneath my feet. This fundamental sense of "otherness" is part of the construction of the ego, or the personal self. According to *Sāṅkhya* philosophy, one of India's oldest dualistic systems, the world is made of two principles: *Puruṣa* (pure consciousness) and *Prakṛti* (material nature). In this vision, touch is an expression of *Prakṛti*—the tangible, changing, sensorial reality. It is how we navigate the world of names and forms.

The five *tanmātras*—subtle elements corresponding to the five senses—form the bridge between spirit and matter. The *sparśa-tanmātra*, or "subtle touch," gives rise to vāyu, the element of air. Vāyu moves, it flows, it is never fixed. Touch, too, is movement—whether in the form of breath brushing against the nostrils or skin against skin. Through touch, we come to know time, change, and life. In the beginning, this knowing separates. But this is only part of the journey.

The *Bhagavad Gita* acknowledges this tension:

"मात्रास्पर्शास्तु कौन्तेय शीतोष्णसुखदुःखदाः।
आगमापायिनोऽनित्यास्तांस्तितिक्षस्व भारत॥"

Mātrā-sparśās tu kaunteya śītoṣṇa-sukha-duḥkha-dāḥ,
Āgamāpāyino'nityās tāṁs titikṣasva bhārata.
(O son of Kunti, the contact between the senses and their objects gives rise to cold and heat, pleasure and pain. These come and go—they are impermanent. Endure them patiently.)

— *Gita 2.14*

Here, Krishna does not deny the experience of touch. Instead, he reframes it. Pleasure and pain, comfort and discomfort—all arise through touch. However, these sensations are transient and do not define the Eternal Self. The soul witnesses, but is not confined by what it feels.

This is a crucial philosophical point: touch is real, but it is not the Real. It is the field of play, the domain where the Self forgets itself in form—but only so it can remember more fully.

From Separation to Communion

If touch begins by affirming separation, its true gift is in guiding us back to union. This is the vision of *Tantra*, a philosophy that embraces the body, senses, and worldly experience not as distractions, but as doorways.

In *Tantric* practice, touch becomes a form of meditation. Whether it is the touch of one's own hands during breath awareness or the sacred touch between partners in conscious intimacy, the experience is slowed down, magnified, and sanctified. The goal is not to escape from the body, but to achieve full presence within it.

In such a presence, something profound occurs. The sense of separateness begins to dissolve. The touch is no longer "me touching you" or "me feeling this." It becomes a single field of awareness in which subject and object merge into one. This is the moment where duality collapses into unity. It is not just physical—it is ontological. The soul remembers that it has never truly been separate from anything.

Patañjali, Yogic Touch, and Inner Perception

In the *Yoga Sūtras* of Patañjali, the journey of *yoga* is described as the gradual stilling of the fluctuations of the mind (*citta-vṛtti-nirodhaḥ*). However, this stilling is not achieved through suppression; it is achieved through the refinement of perception. Touch plays a crucial role here.

The fifth limb of yoga, *pratyāhāra*, is the withdrawal of the senses. This is not a denial of the senses but their inward turning. When we withdraw from external stimulation, the inner touch begins. Yogic traditions describe how, in deep meditation, one may begin to feel sensations within the body that are not caused by external contact—ripples of energy, the movement of breath, or subtle tingling. These are sensations of the subtle body—the *pranic* or energetic body.

According to *Haṭha Yoga* texts, the awakening of *kuṇḍalinī*—the coiled energy at the base of the spine—often begins with a tactile sensation. Practitioners describe warmth, vibration, or movement along the spine or in the space between the brows. This touch is not a metaphor. It is a felt reality, one that bridges the physical and the spiritual.

This is where *yoga*, *tantra*, and *Vedanta* converge: they each recognise that touch is not limited to matter. There is a deeper kind of touch—one that happens when consciousness touches itself, when awareness turns inward and realises it is not the body, not even the mind, but the infinite space in which all sensation arises.

Modern Psychology and the Philosophical Body

Western philosophy and psychology also offer insights into the nature of touch. Phenomenologists, such as Maurice Merleau-Ponty, have emphasised that the body is not an object in the world—it is the subject through which the world is known. To touch is to co-create experience. We do not just "feel" the world—we are shaped by it. Touch transforms the self.

Carl Jung, in his exploration of archetypes and the collective unconscious, spoke of the *anima* and *animus*—the inner feminine and masculine principles within every psyche. In his work, touch—whether literal or symbolic—was a way to engage with these inner energies, to heal the split between self and other. He believed that the longing for intimacy was a longing for wholeness. And in that sense, every touch becomes a gesture toward the divine union within.

In trauma psychology, the concept of somatic memory resonates with these ancient insights. The body stores memory. A gentle hand placed on a trembling shoulder can speak what words cannot. In this light, touch becomes philosophy made flesh—a way of knowing, a way of healing, a way of remembering who we are.

Section 5: From Contact to Communion – Touch and the Path to Enlightenment

Touch begins as sensation, and it ends in realisation. What begins as the contact of skin against skin, of air brushing against flesh, of pressure, warmth, vibration, can, in its most subtle evolution, become the soul touching the Absolute. Enlightenment is not the rejection of sensation—it is the transcendence of identity within it. It is the state in which the seer, the seen, and the seeing become one. And touch, the most primal of senses, becomes a gateway to that union.

The Evolution of Touch

Every newborn is born into a world of touch. At first, it serves as a means of survival. Warmth signifies safety, softness conveys affection, and pressure and rhythm provide reassurance. As the child grows, touch becomes a memory of language, intimacy, comfort, and pain. It teaches boundaries, teaches longing, and teaches trust. But at a certain point in spiritual evolution, the same touch that once defined separation begins to point toward its dissolution.

In the hands of a spiritual seeker, touch becomes a form of awareness. It becomes a mirror. When you hold a cup, do you feel the cup or your fingers against it? When you walk barefoot on the earth, is it you who feels the ground, or is it the earth that feels you? When the wind brushes your face, who is touching whom?

These are not puzzles; they are doorways. The mind cannot answer them, but the body can feel them, and the soul can dissolve into them.

The Great Turning: From Doer to Witness

At the heart of all Eastern spiritual paths is a shift of identity—from the doer to the witness, from *ahamkara* (the ego) to *ātman* (the true Self). This shift can begin in any sense, but touch is perhaps the most direct. Why? Because it demands presence, it is immediate and here.

When we close our eyes and place our hand on our chest, we are not thinking—we are touching. And in that moment, we are both the touched and the toucher. This simple act can become a profound meditation. If we are not the hand, and not the chest, then what are we? We are that which knows the contact. We are the witnesses of sensation.

This witnessing is the path to liberation. The *Kaṭha Upanishad* declares:

"न जायते म्रियते वा कदाचित्। नायं भूत्वा भविता वा न भूयः।"

Na jāyate mriyate vā kadācit, nāyaṁ bhūtvā bhavitā vā na bhūyaḥ.

(The Self is never born, nor does it ever die. It does not come into being nor cease to be.)

The senses cannot touch this Self, and yet it is the knower of all touch. The body may tremble, feel, recoil, or open—but the Self remains still. The journey of enlightenment, then, is not to deny the senses but to root one's identity deeper than them. To know: I feel, but I am not merely the one who feels.

Touch as Bhakti – Devotion in Contact

In devotional traditions, such as Bhakti Yoga, touch is not just awareness—it is love. The divine is not an abstract idea but a presence that can be felt. In the lives of saints and mystics, there are stories of divine embrace, of the *Guru's* hand placed on the disciple's head, of temples where the mere act of touching a stone invokes tears.

The poet-saint *Mira-bai* once wrote: *"I touched His feet and forgot my name."*

This is not a metaphor—it is the language of the soul returning home.

In Bhakti, touch is a form of surrender. When the devotee touches the *murti* (idol), or the feet of the *Guru*, or the sacred soil of a holy place, they are not just contacting an object—they are dissolving the boundaries of self. This touch is communion.

Sparśa Yoga – The Yoga of Touch

In some esoteric *Tantric* traditions, the concept of Sparśa Yoga exists—a form of yoga centred on the subtle power of touch. It is not about physical flexibility or posture, but about refining perception through contact. It may involve sacred gestures (*mudrās*), breath work with internal touch points, or even meditative contact with the body's energy centres.

In this practice, touch is used to awaken awareness in specific parts of the body, not to arouse or manipulate, but to witness. The practitioner learns that the body is not merely flesh; each point on the skin, each organ, and each nerve ending is a doorway into consciousness. One need not travel far to experience the divine. All they need is to be touched by presence.

Stillness That Touches All Things

The culmination of touch is stillness. When the hand no longer moves, when the nerves rest, and when the body is no longer pulled by reaction or desire, a touch arises that is not tactile—it is being itself. This is the touch of *samādhi*—absorption. In deep states of meditation, practitioners report feeling as though they are being touched by light, or touched by nothing, or touched by something vast and gentle beyond name. This is the touch of non-duality, where there is no boundary between subject and object. The senses fall inward, the mind becomes quiet, and the Self realises it was never separate from anything.

In this realisation, the world itself becomes touchable, not the hard edges of the ego, but the soft presence of being. Every breeze, every glance, every heartbeat becomes sacred. The enlightened one walks through the world as if walking through their soul. They touch with reverence, they are touched by silence, they live as a living sensation of the divine.

The Final Shloka: The Touch of Liberation

Let us end with a verse from the *Bṛhadāraṇyaka Upanishad*:

"यत्र त्वस्य सर्वमात्मैवाभूत् तत्केन कं पश्येत्?
कं जिघ्रेत्? कं शृणुयात्?"

Yatra tvasya sarvam ātmaivābhūt tat kena kaṁ paśyet?
Kaṁ jighret? Kaṁ śṛṇuyāt?

(When all has become the Self, then what shall one see, what shall one smell, what shall one hear?)

When all is one, the senses find their resting place—not in withdrawal, but in transcendence. Touch still occurs, but there is neither toucher nor touched. There is only being.

And this… is Enlightenment.

Chapter 4

Sound – Vibrations of the Soul

Section 1: The Sacred Origins of Sound – Nāda, Śabda, and the Voice of Creation

Long before the world had formed, it had sound. Before the stars ignited or the oceans stirred, there was vibration, not of particles, but of potential. A pulse so subtle it carried no weight, yet so vast it birthed galaxies. In Vedic cosmology, this primaeval pulse is called *Nāda*—the unstruck sound, the vibrational essence of creation. Sound, in this view, is not just a sense. It is the seed of the universe.

The Ṛgveda, the oldest of the four Vedas, begins with an invocation to Agni, the fire god, not through vision or offering, but through chanting. Words, when recited in metered tone, become a bridge between earth and heaven. The *ṛṣis* knew this not intellectually but experientially. They meditated, listened deeply, and realised that *śabda* (sound) is the subtle form of Brahman, the eternal principle.

"वाङ् मे मनसि प्रतिष्ठिता मनो मे वाचि प्रतिष्ठितम्।"

Vāṅ me manasi pratiṣṭhitā mano me vāci pratiṣṭhitam

(May speech be established in my mind, and may my mind be established in speech.)

— *Ṛgveda*

This shloka from the Ṛgveda reveals a profound truth: that sound is not outside us. It is an inward illumination. Speech and thought are interwoven. When the mind is still, speech becomes sacred. When speech is aligned with truth, it becomes an offering. And when that offering is made with awareness, it liberates.

The Sacred Origins of Sound – Nāda, Śabda, and the Voice of Creation

Before there was light, there was sound—not as noise, but as subtle vibration, an infinite pulse of potential known in Sanskrit as *Nāda* (नाद). In the mystical cosmology of the Vedas and the Upanishads, sound is not simply an effect of airwaves or vocal cords—it is the first expression of the Absolute, the resonance from which all matter and meaning emerge. The ancients believed that this unstruck sound, *anāhata nāda* (अनाहतनाद), vibrates in the very core of the universe and also in the depths of the soul.

Sound as the First Principle of Creation – Expanded Analysis

In Ṛgveda 10.129, also known as the *Nā sadiya Sūkta,* the Vedic sages attempt to peer into the pre-cosmic void—into the time before time, when neither existence nor non-existence had yet come into being.

"नासदासीन्नो सदासीत्तदानीं नासीद्रजो नो व्योमा परो यत्।"

Nāsad āsīn no sad āsīt tadānīṁ nāsīd rajo no vyomā paro yat
(Then there was neither existence nor non-existence. There was no realm of air, no sky beyond it.)

— *Ṛgveda 10.129.1*

This hymn is not a myth in the modern sense of the word—it is a philosophical meditation on the nature of reality, expressed through the poetic genius of the *ṛṣis* (sages). It speaks of a time before polarity, before dualities such as light and dark, being and non-being, and subject and object.

The seers were not simply speculating on the origin of the universe; they were listening, in profound stillness, to the primordial silence that gives birth to sound. Out of that *śūnya* (void)—not empty, but fertile with potential—arises the first stir, the first vibration. This vibration is *nāda* (नाद) — the inaudible, unstruck sound, or *anāhata.*

From Anāhata to Śabda – The Descent into Form

The concept of *śabda Brahman* (शब्दब्रह्मन्)—the *sound as divine principle*—suggests that the universe is not fundamentally made of particles, but of vibrations. Every element, every atom, every sensation is an echo of that original vibration.

This unmanifest vibration (nāda) becomes manifest sound (śabda) when it begins to differentiate—when duality arises. At that moment, the five elements— space (*ākāśa*), air (*vāyu*), fire (*agni*), water (*apas*), and earth (*pṛthvī*) — come into being through the process known as *pañcīkaraṇa* in Vedantic cosmology.

Thus, sound is first, and form follows. This is not a metaphor but metaphysics. The Vedas declare:

"शब्दो ब्रह्मैव"

Śabdo brahmaiva

(Sound is indeed Brahman.)

This profound phrase captures the non-difference between the Divine and its first expression. Unlike in many religious systems, where creation is shaped by external tools, in the Vedic vision, creation is uttered into existence. *To speak is to create.*

Oṁ (ॐ) as the Living Symbol of this Creation

The syllable Oṁ—described in detail in the *Mandūkya Upanishad*—is the audible form of the inaudible nāda. It is the condensation of all experience into a single syllable, and the syllable itself unfolds the stages of reality:

- **A (अ)** – The waking state (*jāgrat*)
- **U (उ)** – The dreaming state (*svapna*)
- **M (म्)** – The deep sleep state (*suṣupti*)

- **Silence after Oṁ** – The *turiya*, or the state beyond

To chant Oṁ is not just to make a sound—it is to mirror the entire process of creation, sustenance, dissolution, and transcendence.

When the ancients chanted Oṁ, they were not calling out to a god in the sky. They were attuning their consciousness to the vibration from which the cosmos had emerged. They were *rejoining* the song of the universe.

The Mahāpurāṇic Vision of Sound as Divine Will

The Śiva Purāṇa, among others, elaborates on creation through sound in mythic form:

"शिवो नादबिन्दुरूपः, तस्मात् वाणी प्रवर्तते।"

Śivo nāda-bindurūpaḥ, tasmāt vāṇī pravartate

(Śiva is the form of nāda and bindu, from whom speech originates.)

Here, Śiva is *Nāda*, the boundless vibration, and *Bindu*, the point of concentration, the seed. Out of the union of these two arises *Vāk*, the divine voice. In essence, the *Purāṇic* myths preserve the same idea expressed in the Vedas: that sound is not incidental. It is sacred will, the intentional movement of the formless into form.

When *Vāk* speaks, the universe listens—and responds into existence. Thus, creation is a conversation, an unfolding dialogue between *nāda* and *shakti*, between silence and expression, between the Absolute and its dance.

Oṁ – The Sonic Seed of the Infinite (Detailed Expansion)

The *Maṇḍūkya Upaniṣad*, the shortest of the principal *Upaniṣads*, yet the most penetrating, declares in its opening mantra:

"ॐ इत्येतदक्षरं इदं सर्वम्। तस्योपव्याख्यानं भूतं भवद् भविष्यदिति सर्वम् ओङ्कार एव।"

Oṁ ityetad akṣaraṁ idaṁ sarvam. tasyopavyākhyānaṁ bhūtaṁ bhavad bhaviṣyad iti sarvam oṅkāra eva.

(Oṁ—this syllable—is all this. Its explanation: all that was, is, and will be—indeed, everything—is Oṁ alone.)

This is not mere symbolism; it is a direct assertion: Oṁ is the totality of existence—past, present, and future—and also that which transcends time.

Let us now delve into the four parts of Oṁ as outlined in the Upaniṣad:

1. The Sound 'A' (अ) – The Waking State (जागरित अवस्थाः)

"जागरितस्थानो बैष्वानरः 'अ'कारः प्रथमः मात्राः।"

(The waking state, whose consciousness is turned outward and is associated with gross objects, is represented by 'A'.)

- This is the state where the **external world** is perceived through the senses.
- The individual self in this state is called ***Vaiś vānara***, the all-pervading one who experiences through the body and mind.
- It symbolises creation—when the Divine first projects itself outward to manifest the universe.

Spiritual Insight: 'A' arises from the back of the throat, the root of all articulated sound. It is the beginning—not just of words, but of existence. This sound represents our engagement with form, action, doing, and knowing.

2. The Sound 'U' (उ) – The Dreaming State (स्वप्न अवस्थाः)

"स्वप्नस्थानो तैजसः 'उ'कारो द्वितीयः मात्राः।"

(The dreaming state, turned inward, where the subtle body experiences, is represented by 'U'.)

- The self is now ***Taijasa***, the illumined one, experiencing the inner world—dreams, imagination, subconscious processes.
- It represents **sustenance**, the middle phase of the cycle of existence.

- 'U' flows from the middle of the mouth, moving us into the inner world of mind and subtle perception.

Spiritual Insight: This state is more refined than the waking state. Here, the boundaries of form soften, and the soul remembers it is not just a body. It touches intuition, imagination, desire, and karmic residue.

3. The Sound 'M' (म्) – The Deep Sleep State (सुषुप्ति अवस्थाः)

"सुषुप्तस्थानः प्राज्ञो 'म'कारस्तृतीयो मात्रा।"

(The deep sleep state, where there is no desire and no dream, is represented by 'M'.)

- This is the state of *Prājña*, the wise one, enveloped in the bliss of non-differentiation.
- There are no objects, no duality. Consciousness rests in itself.
- 'M' is made by closing the lips. The sound is absorbed, folded inward, symbolising withdrawal.

Spiritual Insight: This is the state of latent awareness, the closest natural experience to the Divine in the unawakened human. The ego dissolves temporarily, leaving no thought, no experience—only potential.

4. The Silence (अमात्रा) – The Fourth State (तुर्यं)

"अमात्रश्चतुर्थः। अव्यवहार्यं प्रपञ्चोपशमं शिवमद्वैतं चतुर्थं मन्यन्ते। स आत्मा स विज्ञेयः॥"

(The fourth, beyond the three, is without parts, indescribable, the cessation of phenomena, all peace, all bliss, non-dual. This is the Self to be realized.)

- This state is called *Turiya*, the fourth, not as another state, but as the background and source of the other three.
- It is not a state of consciousness but consciousness itself, untouched, pure, and unchanging.

Spiritual Insight: This is not a sound, but the silence that follows Oṁ. It is not the absence of sound, but the presence of pure being. This is where Nāda (sound) dissolves into Śūnya (void), and the void reveals fullness.

The Journey of Oṁ through the Body – A Sacred Physiology

When one chants Oṁ mindfully:

- The A vibrates from the navel and lower belly.
- The U rises into the chest and throat, resonating in the heart centre.
- The M closes in the cranial cavity, stimulating the skull, sinuses, and the pineal gland.
- The silence after the sound is felt at the crown, often associated with *Sahasrāra Chakra*, the thousand-petaled lotus of full realisation.

This ascending movement mirrors the path of *Kuṇḍalinī* energy in Yogic philosophy—rising through the *nāḍīs* (energy channels), activating *cakras*, and culminating in spiritual awakening.

From a neuroscientific perspective, chanting Oṁ:

- Activates the vagal nerve, calming the autonomic nervous system.
- Balances the right and left hemispheres of the brain.
- Induces theta and alpha brain waves, states linked with meditative insight and creativity.
- Enhances the functioning of the limbic system, which is the seat of emotions and memory.

Thus, *Oṁ* is the bridge: a vibrational ladder from the gross to the subtle, from the brain to the soul, from personality to presence.

*Sound in the Mahāpurāṇas – Divine Vibration and Sacred Speech*he Mahāpurāṇas are not just stories. They are mythic maps of metaphysical truths, encoded in symbolic narratives that convey deep cosmological and spiritual principles. Among them, the *Śiva Purāṇa*, the *Devī Bhāgavata Purāṇa*, and the *Liṅga Purāṇa* articulate one of the most compelling spiritual revelations: that the universe is not created through material means, but through vibration—through sound —and that *Śabda* (sound) is both the first cause and the ultimate essence.

Śiva – The Silence that Sounds

In the Śiva Purāṇa, Śiva is described as *Nāda Bindu Rūpa* (नाद बिन्दु रूप)—a form that is at once sound and point. These two terms—Nāda (sound) and Bindu (point of concentration)—are not only metaphysical abstractions but experiential realities in yogic practice.

- Nāda represents the vibrational hum of pure awareness, the first stir within the infinite stillness.
- Bindu is the point where form begins, where the formless begins to condense into a seed of possibility.

The *Śiva Purāṇa* says:

"शिवाद्वाचः सृज्यते, वाचः शब्दो भवति। शब्दो विश्वस्य मूलं।"

Śivād vācaḥ sṛjyate, vācaḥ śabdo bhavati. Śabdo viśvasya mūlaṁ.

(From Śiva emerges speech, from speech comes sound. Sound is the root of the universe.)

Here, speech (*vāk*) is not yet verbal expression. It is divine vibration—the creative will of consciousness. And sound (*śabda*) is its first descent into manifestation.

Thus, Śiva does not create through labour. He creates by vibrating silently. His silence is not absence—it is the still fullness that overflows into sound.

The Birth of Vāk – The Goddess of Divine Speech

In both the Ṛgveda and later Purāṇic texts, *Vāk* (वाक्) is personified as a goddess, the daughter of Brahman or Śiva, depending on the tradition, and the mother of all language, poetry, mantra, and sacred recitation.

In Ṛgveda 10.125, Vāk speaks in the first person, not as an abstraction, but as a sovereign deity:

"अहं राष्ट्री संगमनी वसूनां चिकितुषी प्रथमा यज्ञियानाम्।"

Ahaṁ rāṣṭrī saṅgamanī vasūnāṁ cikituṣī prathamā yajñiyānām.

(I am the Sovereign Queen, the gatherer of treasures, the knower of wisdom, first among those worthies of worship.)

This is a bold declaration. Vāk is not secondary to the gods; she is their voice, animating them. Without Vāk, even the gods are mute and powerless.

In the Purāṇic worldview, Vāk is said to emerge from the left side of Śiva, symbolising the birth of Shakti (energy) from pure consciousness. She is thus also Śakti in sonic form—audible energy, sacred resonance.

Vāk is said to exist in four levels, as elaborated in the Devī Bhāgavata Purāṇa and later Tantric texts:

- ***Parā Vāk*** (**परा वाक्**) – The supreme, undifferentiated sound residing in the causal realm.
- ***Paśyantī Vāk*** (**पश्यन्ती वाक्**) – The sound in the intuitive, visionary state.
- ***Madhyamā Vāk*** (**मध्यमा वाक्**) – The sound as thought or subtle internal speech.
- ***Vaikharī Vāk*** (**वैकरी वाक्**) – The expressed, gross speech we hear.

This division is not simply mystical—it reflects the **entire inner process of thought turning into language**. Before we speak, we sense, then we intend, then we shape, then we vocalise.

Vāk, in her journey through these four stages, descends from pure awareness into audible expression.

Spiritual Implications: To Speak is to Invoke

In both the Vedic and Purāṇic traditions, **speech is never merely functional**. It is **sacramental**. Words are sacred because they bind us to vibration. Every utterance is a ripple in the field of consciousness. This is why truthfulness (*satya*) is held as the highest virtue. To speak falsely is not just to lie—it is to distort the vibration of reality.

In the *Purāṇas*, it is said that the mantras, when uttered with sincerity and alignment, can awaken deities, heal the body, and even unravel karma. This is not magic. It is vibrational resonance.

When one recites the name of a deity—say, Śiva or Rāma—it is not just the mind that remembers. The body responds, the nervous system aligns, and the soul stirs. Sound becomes presence. This is *Vāk's* power: to turn language into liberation.

Mythic Symbology – Śiva as the Drum Bearer (Ḍamaru-dhara)

In the *Liṅga Purāṇa* and *Shiva Purāṇa*, Śiva is often depicted holding a *ḍamaru*—a small two-headed drum.

This drum is not symbolic of music alone. It represents the rhythmic pulse of creation and dissolution. According to tradition, the beats of Śiva's *ḍamaru* released the *Maheshvara Sūtras*, a set of 14 phonemes that formed the basis of Sanskrit **grammar**, as systematised later by **Pāṇini** in the *Aṣṭādhyāyī*.

"नादरूपं हरिं ध्यायेत् नादबिन्दुं महेश्वरम्।"

Nādarūpaṁ hariṁ dhyāyet nāda-binduṁ maheśvaram

(Meditate on Hari in the form of sound, and on Śiva as the bindu of that nāda.)

This is why language, grammar, mantra, and sound are treated as manifestations of divinity. To study sound is to worship, to chant with intention is to co-create, to listen deeply is to remember our origin in vibration.

The Soteriological Role of Sound–Mantra as a Path to *Mokṣa*

From the Vedas to the Purāṇas, the purpose of sacred sound is not only to describe creation, but to liberate the soul from illusion. This is why mantras—sound formulas composed of *bija* (seed syllables)—are seen as vehicles of *mokṣa* (मोक्ष), liberation.

The sound itself is the path. No belief is necessary. If the mantra is recited with full attention and a pure heart, its vibration enters the subtle body, realigns the energy centres (chakras), stills the mind, and awakens the inner listener—the ātman.

This belief is not superstition. Sound affects matter. In modern science, the study of cymatics shows how sound waves create patterns in physical materials. Chanting alters the brain's electromagnetic fields, synchronising neural oscillations. But beyond the physical, it shifts the very field of consciousness. The mantra is not just heard—it is lived.

The Sacred Use of Hearing – Śravaṇa as a Spiritual Practice

In the Jnana Yoga tradition of the Upanishads, the first step toward realisation is *śravaṇa* (श्रवण)—*deep listening*. This is not passive hearing, but an active, intentional openness to truth. One listens to the teacher, to the *śāstra* (scriptures), and eventually, to the inner sound of the Self.

The ***Chāndogya Upanishad*** declares:

"सर्वं खल्विदं ब्रह्म तज्जलानिति शान्त उपासीत।"

Sarvaṁ khalvidaṁ brahma tajjalāniti śānta upāsīta

(All this is indeed Brahman. From it, it is born, in it it merges, in it it breathes. Know this and become still.)

— *Chāndogya Upanishad 3.14.1*

This verse, too, is heard—not just read or known—but listened to in silence, where the words become vibration, then recognition, then silence again. It is through this process that the soul begins to awaken—first sound, then stillness and then Self.

Section 2: Auditory Alchemy – The Physiology of Hearing and the Nervous System

Sound is not just vibration in the air—it is a biological journey, a neural symphony, and a spiritual experience. When a sound wave travels through the world and enters the ear, it does not merely cause a mechanical response—it awakens memory, evokes emotion, and at times, unlocks transcendence. In the context of Indian philosophy, this physiological process is not separate from the spiritual—it is a living bridge between matter and consciousness, between outer vibration and inner awareness.

Let us now explore, in a step-by-step yet fluid narrative, how the body perceives sound, how the brain decodes it, and how the soul responds.

The Tympanic Membrane – Where Vibration Enters the Body

As sound waves travel through the carefully curved architecture of the outer ear, they culminate their journey at a delicate, almost invisible barrier: the tympanic membrane, commonly known as the eardrum. This fragile, translucent membrane is stretched tightly across the end of the auditory canal, forming the threshold where the external world meets the inner sanctum of the human body. It is here, in the trembling dance of the eardrum, that sound first truly **touches** us.

The tympanic membrane is not merely a passive surface; it is a living, breathing entity that responds to the subtlest caress of moving air. When a sound wave strikes the membrane, it causes an intricate, microscopic vibration that precisely mirrors the pattern and rhythm of the incoming wave. A whisper brushes the membrane with gentle ripples; a thunderclap hammers against it with dramatic force. In both cases, the eardrum does not distort or interpret—it **listens perfectly**, allowing itself to be affected by the vibration without resistance. It becomes an instrument of surrender, much like the soul in deep meditation, open and receptive to the cosmic symphony.

Structurally, the tympanic membrane is layered with incredible precision. Its outer surface is continuous with the skin of the auditory canal; its inner surface merges with the mucous membrane of the middle ear, and between these two lies a fibrous layer that provides both strength and flexibility. This delicate construction allows the eardrum to withstand the pressure of everyday sounds while remaining exquisitely sensitive to subtle frequencies. It is a marvel of biological engineering, crafted not merely to survive, but to **feel**—to translate invisible waves into the language of the body.

The sacredness of the tympanic membrane can be compared to the veil of the temple in ancient traditions—a thin but powerful boundary separating the profane from the sacred. Just as a seeker steps through the temple gates to approach the divine, sound must pass through the eardrum to enter the inner corridors of perception. The tympanic membrane is thus not only a physiological necessity; it is a symbolic gateway, a vibrating portal where the external and internal worlds intertwine.

The Vedas frequently refer to the senses as sacred horses pulling the chariot of the body, guided by the mind and the soul. In this imagery, the ear—beginning with the tympanic membrane—is the sacred field where the horses first make contact with the ground. The *Bhagavad Gita* hints at this interaction when Krishna tells Arjuna that the wise one sees the senses, sense-objects, and consciousness not as separate, but as a single flow of experience. In the same way, when sound touches the eardrum, it does not remain an "outside" force. It becomes part of us, entering the body's living matrix.

From a modern scientific perspective, the tympanic membrane serves as a master translator, converting the kinetic energy of sound waves—energy that travels through air at approximately 340 meters per second—into mechanical energy that can then be amplified and processed further. If the membrane were too loose, it would fail to transmit subtle sounds; if it were too rigid, it would shatter under loud vibrations. Its tension is maintained by tiny muscles in the middle ear, especially the tensor tympani and the stapedius, which can adjust their tautness in real time, protecting the inner ear from damage while allowing it to remain sensitive to whispers of beauty.

Interestingly, the tympanic membrane is not a solitary listener. It works in harmony with the ossicles, the three small bones of the middle ear, to create a mechanical advantage that amplifies sound energy almost twentyfold before it reaches the inner ear. This teamwork between the eardrum and the bones behind it can be seen as an allegory for the spiritual journey: no one element—neither body, mind, nor spirit—operates alone. All must move together, tuned to the sacred rhythm, if actual hearing and ultimately true awakening are to occur.

Spiritually speaking, the tympanic membrane teaches an invaluable lesson: receptivity is not weakness; it is strength. To allow oneself to be touched deeply by experience, to vibrate in sympathy with the world around us without losing one's essential nature, is a mark of maturity and wisdom. The eardrum does not control the sounds it receives, but neither does it collapse under their weight. It translates without judgment. It offers itself fully without losing its integrity. This is the path of the seeker as well—to remain open yet steady, touched but not torn, resonant but not reactive.

When a yogi listens to the inner nāda during meditation—the subtle hum that rises in profound stillness—they are tuning in to this vibrational mystery. The eardrum itself, though physically still, seems to mirror this internal sound. It is as if, once the outer world becomes silent, the eardrum begins to hear the original vibration from which all creation sprang. In this profound silence, the eardrum ceases to be a barrier and becomes a bridge, linking the world of form with the formless truth.

Thus, the tympanic membrane, humble and hidden though it may be, is one of the most profound sites of spiritual potential within the human body. It is here that sound ceases to be a distant phenomenon and becomes a felt experience. It is here that vibration enters flesh, that the song of existence is invited into the temple of the body. And it is here, if we listen carefully enough, that the first echoes of enlightenment begin to resound.

The Middle Ear Bones – The Orchestra of Transmission

Beyond the vibrating tympanic membrane lies a hidden chamber of great subtlety and significance—the middle ear, home to the smallest bones in the human body, yet among the most profound in function and symbolism. Nestled within this tiny air-filled cavity are the ossicles: the malleus, the incus, and the stapes—known in English as the hammer, the anvil, and the stirrup. Though minuscule, these three bones form a delicate mechanical orchestra, finely attuned to receive the message of vibration and carry it forward with amplified grace and precision.

When the tympanic membrane responds to a sound wave, it does not vibrate in isolation—it sends its energy directly to the malleus, which is fused to the inner surface of the membrane. The malleus rocks in time with the eardrum, transferring its movement to the incus, which acts as a silent intermediary. The incus, in turn, presses against the stapes, which is positioned at the oval window, the gateway into the fluid-filled inner ear. With this final motion, the stapes transmits the mechanical pulse into the dense fluid of the cochlea, initiating the inner alchemy that will ultimately result in hearing.

This process of mechanical conduction is not only exquisitely coordinated—it is miraculous. The bones amplify the vibration of sound over 20 times, allowing the energy of a whisper or a distant bell to pass from the air into the fluid medium of the inner ear without loss. This is no ordinary engineering feat. It is a transmutation of elements, a symbolic movement from lightness to density, from air to water, from outer noise to inner knowing. These three bones, held in eternal conversation, act as bridges—not only anatomically but spiritually. They link the ephemeral to the substantial, the outer world to the inner temple of perception.

From the spiritual perspective, the three ossicles reflect a deeper triad found in many traditions. In Vedantic philosophy, we find the sacred trinity of *Sat* (truth), *Chit* (consciousness), and *Ānanda* (bliss). In yogic systems, we encounter the three *guṇas*—*sattva, rajas,* and *tamas*—which define the energetic quality of all existence. In the structure of the mind, we speak of *manas* (mind), *buddhi* (intellect), and *ahaṁkāra* (ego). These trinities are not separate entities; they work together in balance and resonance, just like the ossicles. No single part dominates; each listens and responds. This harmony is the key to transformation.

Symbolically, the malleus, being directly connected to the eardrum, may be likened to *manas,* the reactive mind that first receives impressions from the world. The incus, situated between the two extremes, can be seen as *buddhi,* the discerning intelligence that refines and stabilises. Finally, the stapes, which conveys the final vibration into the inner sanctum of the cochlea, can be compared to *ātmā*. This individualised consciousness connects the experience back to the Self. In this way, every sound we hear is not just passing through physical structures—it is travelling through layers of awareness, each one contributing to the evolution of perception.

The sacred geometry of the ossicles, arranged in a chain of connection, reminds us of the importance of continuity. If even one bone is damaged, if one connection is broken, the entire process falters. This teaches a valuable spiritual lesson: transmission requires trust and alignment. Just as sound must flow seamlessly through the ossicles to be perceived as meaningful, so too must divine wisdom pass through the subtle layers of our being—body, breath, emotion, intellect—without resistance, without distortion. If any link is closed by fear, distraction, or attachment, the transmission becomes muffled. But if the whole system is attuned, the soul hears clearly.

Moreover, the ossicles are suspended within the middle ear by a series of ligaments and muscles, including the tensor tympani and the stapedius, the smallest skeletal muscle in the human body. These muscles act as protectors and regulators, tightening in response to loud or sudden noises to prevent damage to the inner ear. This mechanism, known as the acoustic reflex, serves as both a shield and a filter, protecting the sanctity of perception and allowing only what is necessary to pass through. Spiritually, this echoes the concept of *pratyāhāra*, the yogic discipline of sense withdrawal. The senses are not to be destroyed, but to be governed—guarded—not by suppression, but by wisdom. The inner listener chooses which vibrations to admit and which to soften.

From a psycho-emotional perspective, the ossicles also mirror how we process experience. The world sends its messages through sound, speech, tone, and we receive them not merely as information, but as vibrations. These vibrations travel through our inner bones, evoking memories, judgments, and longings. Some sounds pass through us freely, others lodge and echo. The bones within the ear remember how to vibrate—but the soul within the heart must learn how to listen.

In silence, too, the ossicles have their role. When no sound arrives from the world, they rest. But in deep meditation, when the practitioner begins to hear the subtle anāhata nāda, the unstruck sound, the ossicles seem to awaken again, not physically, but energetically. Some yogis report a sense of inner pulsation, a rhythm that beats behind the ears, a hum that has no origin. In these moments, the ossicles are not simply conduits for outer sound—they become instruments of inner music, tuning themselves to the divine frequency that vibrates in all things.

Thus, the ossicles, while tiny in form, carry the architecture of transformation. They represent the principle of receiving, refining, and transmitting, which lies at the heart of all sacred processes—whether in sound, thought, or the soul's journey toward truth. They remind us that what is small can be essential, and that behind every vibration lies a chain of hidden devotion.

Through them, we come to know that listening is not a passive act. It is active participation in the sacred. The bones of the middle ear do not simply conduct—they co-create the experience of sound. And in that co-creation, they offer us a glimpse of how the Divine listens to us—not with thunder or force, but through the quiet transmission of presence, bone to bone, soul to soul, silence to song.

The Ossicles – The Silent Musicians of the Sacred Symphony

Hidden in the tiny vault of the middle ear, suspended in air yet bound in delicate unity, lie three of the most extraordinary structures of the human body: the **ossicles**. Though they are the smallest bones in the entire anatomy—so small that all three can fit on a fingernail—they wield a power disproportionate to their size. They are not inert levers or simple mechanical tools; they are living bridges, carrying the song of the universe from the external world into the inner sanctum of human consciousness. Without them, the vibrations collected by the tympanic membrane would crash against the boundaries of flesh and die unheard. Because of them, vibration becomes resonance, and resonance becomes knowing.

The journey begins with the malleus, aptly named the hammer, whose long handle is fused intimately to the inner surface of the tympanic membrane. When the eardrum trembles in response to sound, the malleus moves with it in perfect sympathy. It does not delay, hesitate, or distort; it surrenders to the pulse with absolute fidelity. It accepts the touch of the world without judgment and begins the sacred act of conduction. This unhesitating reception mirrors the soul's ideal state—responsive to the truth of experience, yet unwavering.

The incus, or anvil, follows next. Positioned between the malleus and the stapes, it forms a quiet bridge, receiving vibrations from the malleus and passing them onward. The incus does not add to or subtract from the message; it refines it, stabilises it, and ensures its faithful transmission. Symbolically, the incus represents discernment—*buddhi*—the capacity to understand without distortion, to balance the sensory input before it moves deeper into being. In a world often clouded by reaction and haste, the incus reminds us of the virtue of silent witnessing, of the strength found in stillness.

The stapes, the stirrup, completes the chain. Shaped like an ancient tuning fork or a gateway, it stands as the final guardian before sound crosses from the airy world of vibration into the watery realm of the cochlea. With the soft yet determined press of its footplate against the oval window, the stapes initiates the next stage of the alchemy. Its movement is so precise, so subtle, that even the faintest whisper of energy is transformed and conveyed. The stapes is not merely the end of the chain—it is the threshold keeper, the one who ensures that only a purified, amplified vibration reaches the holy spiral within.

The union of these three bones is a masterpiece of evolutionary craftsmanship. Together, they amplify the incoming sound energy by almost 22 times, overcoming the significant challenge of transmitting a vibration from the air-filled middle ear into the denser fluid of the inner ear. In physical terms, this is known as impedance matching, a necessary adaptation without which the rich symphony of the world would be little more than a murmur. In spiritual terms, it is a lesson in proper transmission—the ability to carry truth across thresholds of difference, from subtle to gross, from spirit to matter, from soul to mind.

The ossicles are held in dynamic suspension by the tensor tympani and stapedius muscles, which adjust tension on the bones in response to incoming sound. When a loud noise is detected, these muscles contract reflexively, dampening the movement of the bones and protecting the delicate structures of the inner ear from damage. This acoustic reflex embodies the sacred balance between openness and protection. It reminds us that spiritual listening is not naive absorption of all sounds, but conscious discernment—a knowing of when to open fully, and when to shield the inner sanctum to preserve its sanctity.

Interestingly, these middle ear structures not only serve to amplify but also filter and prioritise. Human sensitivity is most significant in the frequency range of human speech, particularly between 2,000 and 5,000 Hertz. This selective amplification reflects an evolutionary truth: Connection, the ability to hear and be heard, is fundamental to survival and flourishing. From a spiritual perspective, it suggests that at the heart of existence is not isolation, but relationship. The ossicles thus become ministers of connection, bearing each vibration with care, delivering it faithfully across realms.

When seen through the eye of sacred anatomy, the ossicles form a triadic structure like the *trishula*—the three-pronged spear carried by Lord Śiva. The trishula represents creation, preservation, and dissolution; past, present, and future; body, mind, and spirit. Similarly, the malleus, incus, and stapes together orchestrate the journey of sound from ephemeral vibration to embodied awareness. They are the soul's first disciples, receiving the wordless hymns of existence and preparing them for the inner sanctuary where meaning is born.

In *Tantric* traditions, the transformation of nāda (sound) into an experience of bliss (*ānanda*) is central to spiritual realisation. Just as the primal vibration descends into gross matter through a hierarchy of energies—*nāda* to *bindu* to *mantra*—so too does external sound descend through the ossicles into the fluid temple of the cochlea. Each bone performs its role with humility and grace, participating silently in a rite that transforms mere movement of air into profound emotional, psychological, and spiritual resonance.

Moreover, the ossicles perform their ministry in silence. They do not produce sound; they conduct it. They do not seek attention; they enable attention. In this, they model the path of the true spiritual aspirant: to serve the transmission of wisdom without ego, to enable connection without needing to be seen, to resonate with the truth without demanding recognition.

Thus, the malleus, incus, and stapes are not merely mechanical entities; they are priests of the inner temple, guardians of the threshold where the external world touches the soul. Every time a sound reaches us—whether the laughter of a child, the murmur of a river, or the sacred syllable Oṁ—it is these silent servants who lift it, carry it, and offer it to the higher centres of consciousness. They remind us that in every act of authentic listening, something profound occurs: we do not merely hear the world; we are touched by it, transformed by it, and if we listen deeply enough, liberated through it.

The Cochlea and Inner Ear – The Spiral Temple of Sound

Beyond the oval window, where the delicate foot of the stapes presses its rhythmic pulse, lies one of the most magnificent and mysterious structures in the human body: the **cochlea**. Shaped like a coiled spiral, reminiscent of the sacred geometry found in the structure of galaxies, seashells, and whirlpools, the cochlea is not merely an anatomical feature—it is a temple of transformation. In this mystical chamber, mechanical vibration becomes the conscious experience of sound. It is in this secret spiral that the journey of external energy is finally received, interpreted, and ultimately recognised as part of the soul's inner world.

The cochlea itself is a tiny structure, no larger than a small garden snail, yet it contains an intricate labyrinth of fluid-filled canals and chambers. It is divided into three main ducts—the scala vestibuli, scala media, and scala tympani—separated by delicate membranes that vibrate in response to the movements initiated by the stapes. Within the scala media lies the organ of Corti, the true heart of the cochlea, where thousands of microscopic hair cells are arranged in exquisite rows along the basilar membrane. These hair cells are the sentinels of perception, standing like silent monks in the sacred cloister of hearing, awaiting the arrival of the invisible pilgrim—sound.

When the cochlear fluid moves, it causes the basilar membrane to ripple. These ripples are not uniform; each segment of the membrane is tuned to a specific frequency, much like the strings of a finely crafted instrument. Higher frequencies cause vibration near the base of the cochlea, while lower frequencies resonate near the apex, deep within the spiral's heart. Thus, the cochlea performs a miraculous act of tonotopic mapping—a perfect translation of frequency into place. Every note we hear, every whisper and roar, is laid out along this spiral map, carved into the living flesh of perception.

The hair cells embedded in the organ of Corti do more than move; they convert mechanical energy into electrochemical signals. When their delicate cilia bend under the fluid's ripple, they open ion channels that initiate a cascade of neural impulses. These signals travel through the auditory nerve, heading first to the brainstem, then the thalamus, and finally to the auditory cortex, where sound becomes conscious awareness. In this astonishing alchemy, a pressure wave that began as a disturbance in the air becomes the rich texture of human experience—music, speech, laughter, sorrow, silence.

From a spiritual perspective, the cochlea is much more than a biological structure. Its spiral shape holds profound symbolic significance. In the wisdom traditions of the world, the spiral represents evolution and involution —the journey outward into manifestation and the return inward to the source. In yogic cosmology, the spiral mirrors the *kundalinī* energy coiled at the base of the spine, awaiting awakening. Just as *kundalinī* rises through the nāḍīs and cakras, bringing about spiritual illumination, so too does sound spiral inward through the cochlea, awakening layers of meaning, emotion, and memory within the seeker.

The cochlea's spiral can also be seen as a microcosm of the soul's journey through life. In the beginning, the sounds we hear are simple, basic, primal—the cry of the mother, the drumbeat of the earth. As we spiral deeper into life, we encounter increasingly complex sounds—language, music, poetry, and sacred chants. If we continue to listen with the ears of the heart, we spiral even deeper, into the silent music behind all sounds, into the nāda anāhata—the unstruck sound. This eternal resonance is the voice of Brahman itself.

Within the cochlea, the hair cells themselves perform the spiritual act of surrender. They do not resist the movement of the fluid; they bend, yield, and open. They offer themselves fully to the wave that moves through them, and in that offering, they become conduits for the transmission of life. If even a few hair cells are damaged, specific frequencies are lost to hearing forever. Thus, the lesson of the cochlea is clear: receptivity is sacred, and true transformation requires total presence, total offering, total listening.

The sacred texts of India often describe creation itself as a vibration, a song of being. The Ṛgveda speaks of the cosmic order, or ṛta, established through the hymns and chants of the gods. The Śiva Purāṇa describes Śiva playing the ḍamaru drum, whose beats create the rhythms of time and space. In the cochlea, this cosmic music is mirrored. Each ripple of the basilar membrane is a note in the great symphony of existence; each hair cell is a devoted instrument in the eternal orchestra of life. When we hear, truly hear, we are not merely detecting sound—we are participating in creation's unfolding.

The cochlea also teaches the importance of balance, sharing space within the inner ear with the vestibular system, which governs equilibrium and orientation. In the inner sanctum of hearing, sound and balance are inseparable. This is not incidental; it reflects a profound metaphysical truth that true hearing—actual reception of the Divine—requires inner stability. The seeker must not be buffeted by every external noise, but must stand centred, rooted, and receptive. Sound is sacred, but it is sacred only to those whose hearts are steady, whose awareness is anchored.

In moments of deep meditation, when the senses are drawn inward and the mind becomes still, practitioners often report hearing an inner sound —a subtle hum or ringing — that seems to arise not from the outer world but from within. This experience, known as *nāda anubhava*, is considered a milestone on the path to *samādhi*. It is the soul's hearing of its resonance with the Absolute. And the physical ear, the cochlea, has prepared the way for this experience through a lifetime of listening, bearing the music of the world with devotion and grace.

Thus, the cochlea is not merely a receiver of sound. It is the womb of hearing, the spiral temple where vibration is conceived into meaning, where the outer becomes inner, and where the noise of the world can, if attended with reverence, be transformed into the song of the Self. Every time we hear a sound, it is not just an event; it is a reminder. We are not separate. We are instruments in the symphony of being. The music has always been playing. The cochlea, in its silent spiral, waits patiently for us to listen—not with the ears alone, but with the soul.

The Auditory Pathway to the Brain – The Ascension of Sound into Consciousness

When the sacred river of vibration leaves the cochlea, it does not end its journey; it begins a higher ascent. The electrical impulses generated by the bending of tiny hair cells flow upward through the auditory nerve, a silver thread connecting the spiral temple of the ear to the palace of the mind. But this is not a mechanical transmission. It is a pilgrimage of perception, a sacred climb through stations of refinement, where raw sound is sculpted into meaning, memory, emotion, and transcendence.

The first station on this ascending path is the cochlear nuclei, embedded deep within the brainstem. Here, the river of sound splits and branches, sending signals to both sides of the brain. This bilateral sharing of information is no accident; it ensures that we hear in stereophony, a subtle, dynamic field that allows us to sense depth, location, and texture in the soundscape around us. Spiritually, this reflects the ancient principle of dvandva, the pairs of opposites—left and right, self and other, inner and outer—that must be harmonised to realise unity.

From the cochlear nuclei, the auditory signals ascend to the superior olivary complex, where the brain begins to discern the timing and intensity differences between the two ears. This binaural comparison enables us to locate sound in space, determining whether a voice calls from the east or a river sings to the west. But more than physical orientation, this localisation reflects the awakening of discrimination (*viveka*)—the ability to know where we are in relation to the vibrations that move through us.

Further up the sacred path, the signals reach the inferior colliculus, a midbrain structure that integrates auditory reflexes and startle responses. It is here that sound begins to acquire urgency, emotional weight, or calm reassurance. Some sounds trigger the sympathetic nervous system into alertness; others ease us into parasympathetic relaxation. In the spiritual context, this stage serves as the testing ground for *vairāgya*, or detachment. Can the seeker hear the sounds of the world without being enslaved by them? Can one respond to vibration without becoming entangled in reaction?

The final station before entering conscious awareness is the medial geniculate body of the thalamus. This is the great relay centre, the doorkeeper of sensory input, deciding what will be allowed to reach the seat of knowing, the cerebral cortex. Only those vibrations that bear sufficient significance, that resonate deeply enough, are permitted to pass through. This mirrors the yogic teaching of *pratyāhāra*, the withdrawal and refinement of sensory currents, a conscious process that filters distractions and cultivates inner focus.

At last, the river of sound flows into the primary auditory cortex in the temporal lobes of the brain. Here, vibration is no longer mere movement. It becomes music, language, meaning, and memory. It becomes the laugh of a beloved, the cry of a newborn, the chant of a mantra, the silent hum of eternity. Through the miraculous workings of the brain, sound ascends from matter into mind, and from mind into soul.

The Vedic sages knew this truth in their most profound meditation. They taught that the journey of sound is not complete until it awakens the inner ear, the ear of the heart, the *śrotraṁ Brahma*—the hearing that is Brahman itself.

The ancient Śaiva scriptures celebrate this inner hearing with hymns that blend devotion and realisation. One such revered hymn is the Śivamānasa Pūjā, a mental worship of Lord Śiva composed by Śrī Śaṅkarācārya. Let us hear its beginning:

In Devanagari (as you wrote):

“रत्नैः कल्पितमासनं हिमजलैः स्नानं च दिव्याम्बरं
नानारत्नविभूषितं मृगमदामोदाङ्कितं चन्दनम्।
जातीचम्पकबिल्वपत्ररचितं पुष्पं च धूपं तथा
दीपं देव दयानिधे पशुपते हृत्कल्पितं गृह्यताम्॥”

Meaning in English:

“O compassionate Lord Śiva, Lord of all beings, I offer you in my heart a throne crafted with precious gems, a sacred bath with pure, cool water, divine garments, ornaments adorned with many precious jewels, fragrant sandal paste scented with musk, flowers made from jasmine, champaka, and bilva leaves, along with sacred incense and lit lamps. Please accept this worship, lovingly created within my heart.”

This hymn reveals a powerful truth: even when outer action ceases, inner vibration continues. Even if the body is still, the mind sings, the soul worships. Inner sound—the true *śabda*—rises when the outer noise falls silent.

Similarly, the Rudraṁ, a revered portion of the Yajurveda, praises the Lord who is found in every sound, in every tremor of the universe:

"नमः शम्भवाय च मयोभवाय च। नमः शङ्कराय च मयस्कराय च।"

Namaḥ śambhavāya ca mayobhavāya ca, namaḥ śaṅkarāya ca mayaskarāya ca

Meaning:

"Salutations to Him who is Śambhu, the Source of Bliss. Salutations to Him who brings Auspiciousness and Joy."

Here, the mantra becomes a vibration that harmonises the listener with the inner Śiva, the eternal witness of all sound. Thus, the journey of sound from the cochlea to the cortex is not merely a biological process. It is a *sādhana*, a spiritual practice, by which the soul is continually offered the chance to awaken. Every sound, rightly heard, is a call to presence. Every vibration, rightly received, is an invitation to liberation.

When the mind finally listens not only to external sounds but to the subtle music of its source, the seeker discovers the most profound truth: Sound and Silence are one. The world is vibrating, and so is the soul. Śiva dances in both.

Section 3: Vibration and Vision – Philosophical Interpretations of Sound across Darśanas and Sacred Texts

Sound, in the eyes of the ancient Indian philosophers, is never an isolated phenomenon. It is not merely the disturbance of air, nor simply a tool for communication. In the deepest vision of the Darśanas—the great philosophical systems of India—sound is woven into the very fabric of reality. It is the thread *(sūtra)* by which the cosmos is stitched together, the pulse *(spanda)* that makes the inert vibrant, the call *(āhvāna)* that summons the soul from sleep into remembrance.

The *Sāṅkhya Darśana*, among the oldest philosophical systems, speaks of tanmātras, the subtle elements from which the gross elements arise. Sound is linked with *ākāśa* (space), the first of the five elements to emerge from the primordial *prakṛiti*, the unmanifest nature. Without space, there can be no vibration; without vibration, there can be no experience. Thus, in Sāṅkhya, sound is not a by-product—it is the first expression of differentiation, the earliest whisper of the many from the One.

In *Vedānta*, the most refined culmination of Indian thought, sound is seen as Brahman in motion. The *Taittirīya* ***Upaniṣad*** declares:

"वाचो हि आत्मा।"

Vāco hi ātmā.

(Speech, verily, is the Self.)

Here, "speech" does not mean mere utterance, but the living vibration that underlies both sound and silence. The Self is not mute emptiness; it is full, resounding, humming with unseen music. When the wise speak of Brahman as "not this, not that," they do not mean absence but a fullness that cannot be captured in ordinary sound, a fullness felt in the very breath between syllables, in the silence that births every word.

The *Mīmāṁsā Darśana*, which focuses on the philosophy of ritual, elevates sound to the status of divinity itself. For *Mīmāṁsakas*, the Vedic mantras are eternal and self-existent; they were not composed by human beings, but are *apauruṣeya*, not of mortal origin. The mantras exist eternally in the realm of sound, waiting to be accessed, recited, and thus reconnected to the Divine Order (ṛta). Here, sound is not communication; it is cosmic maintenance. Chanting is not prayer—it is participation in the very rhythm that sustains existence.

The Yoga Darśana, compiled by Patañjali, gives an even subtler insight. The Yoga Sūtras speak of nāda—inner sound—as a signpost on the path to *samādhi*, the union with the Self. In deep meditation, the yogi hears not external noise, but an inner resonance that calls the consciousness home. Patañjali describes the inner hearing thus:

"प्रत्याहारश्च मनसः स्वस्वरूपानुकार इवेन्द्रियाणाम्।"

Pratyāhāraśca manasaḥ svasvarūpānukāra iveṅdriyāṇām.

(Pratyāhāra is the withdrawal of the senses, in the manner of their assimilation into the mind's nature.)

When the senses turn inward, the ears no longer chase external sounds. Instead, they become attuned to the primal vibration—the unstruck sound (anāhata nāda)—that sings continuously in the heart of all being. This inner sound is not a metaphor; it is a mystical experience known to *yogis* across centuries, a gateway to transcendence through vibration.

The *Śaiva Darśanas*, especially the tradition of Kashmir Śaivism, take the role of sound even deeper. In the *Spanda **Kārikā***, a key text, it is said:

"न स्पन्दं विहाय स्थिरं किञ्चिदस्ति।"

Na spandaṁ vihāya sthiraṁ kiñcid asti.

(Nothing exists without spanda, the throb or vibration.)

Here, *spanda* is the sacred vibration, the primal quiver that is not different from Śiva Himself. Existence is not a static being; it is pulsation, a living tremour of consciousness delighting in itself. Every sound heard in the world, from the rustling of leaves to the chant of a mantra, is an echo of this primal spanda. The act of truly hearing thus becomes an act of recognising Śiva vibrating as the world.

In the *Mahāpurāṇas*, particularly the *Liṅga Purāṇa* and *Śiva Purāṇa*, sound is celebrated in the form of Śiva Nāda, the cosmic drumbeat that creates and dissolves worlds. The beating of Śiva's *ḍamaru* at the end of his *Tāṇḍava* dance is said to have released the *Maheshvara Sūtras*, fourteen sacred sounds from which the Sanskrit language is believed to have originated. Each beat is not only a pulse of creation but a call to liberation.

The *Śiva Mahimna Stotra*, a grand hymn glorifying Lord Śiva, sings:

"त्वमपि जगतां नाथाः पश्यसि स्वात्मरूपं।"

Tvam api jagatāṁ nāthāḥ paśyasi svātmarūpaṁ.

(You, O Lord of the worlds, see only Your Self in all creation.)

Sound, in this vision, is the mirror Śiva holds to himself. To hear deeply is not merely to perceive phenomena—it is to perceive the Self reflecting itself, rejoicing in its resonance, remembering its eternal dance.

Thus, in every *Darśana*, from the analytic *Sāṅkhya* to the ecstatic *Śaiva*, sound is never trivial. It is the primordial medium, the living bridge, the golden thread between matter and spirit, between the seen and the unseen. To listen deeply—to listen not only with the physical ears but with the inner ear of awareness—is to step onto the bridge that leads from individual vibration to universal consciousness, from echoes of separation to the silence of unity.

Section 4: Sound, Emotion, and Memory – The Soul's Inner Echoes

There is a sound that does not end when the ears stop listening — a sound that lingers in the folds of memory, in the warmth of tears, and in the tremble of the body when no words are spoken. This sound is not heard—it is felt. It is remembered not by the brain, but by the soul. It arises not from the external world, but from the meeting point of experience and meaning. This is the sound that lives within emotion, that travels through the corridors of memory, and that binds consciousness to its most profound truths.

Biologically, every sound that enters the ear and reaches the auditory cortex does not stop at identification. A voice, a melody, a cry—it is not only labelled or interpreted. It is sent, through intricate pathways of white matter, to the limbic system, the emotional core of the brain. Here, sound meets emotion, and what was previously just a pattern of waves becomes joy, grief, longing, or devotion. The amygdala, that almond-shaped sentinel of feeling, deciphers the emotional colour of every vibration. The hippocampus, the scribe of memory, ties each sound to time, place, and feeling. And the hypothalamus, the master of hormonal responses, translates vibration into the body's language—heartbeat, breath, and tears.

It is for this reason that a mother's voice can calm a child without logic, that a sacred chant, heard after decades of silence, can evoke tears in an old man who has forgotten everything but his God, that a *rāga* played in the twilight can awaken a memory never consciously held, yet known in the bones. Sound bypasses intellect and enters directly into the emotional field, a truth ancient India understood with profound sensitivity.

The sages of the Upanishads knew this when they declared:
"यथा सोम्या मधु मधुकृतो निःश्रित्यैकतं गतं, यथातत्तैः न विदुः तदहमेवेदं सर्वम्।"
Yathā somyā madhu madhukṛto niḥśṛtyaikatāṁ gataṁ, yathā tat-

taiḥ na viduḥ tad aham evedaṁ sarvam.
(As the honey, extracted by bees from different trees, becomes the same, so too all beings, though arising from different paths, merge into the Self without knowing they are the same.)

— *Chandogya Upanishad 6.9.1*

Just as many bees gather nectar from various flowers to produce one honey, so do our emotional experiences—joys, losses, sounds, and silences—gather within us, forming a single living memory of the Self. The sounds that pass through our lives do not fade; they become part of our internal resonance, becoming *vāsanās*—subtle impressions that condition how we respond to the present. This is why a sacred mantra, recited daily, does not just calm the mind—it recalibrates the emotional body, cleansing memory, softening reaction, purifying perception.

In Ayurveda, the connection between sound and emotion is well understood. Each *doṣa*—*vāta*, *pitta*, *kapha*—uniquely responds to vibration. *Vāta*, made of air and ether, is soothed by soft, rhythmic sounds and aggravated by harsh, erratic ones. *Pitta*, of fire and water, responds to melody and devotion, and flares with aggressive tone or loudness. *Kapha*, composed of earth and water, is moved by uplifting, stimulating vibrations that awaken its inertia. Thus, sound becomes medicine, not just for the body, but also for the emotional constitution.

This sacred science of sound and healing finds full expression in the Nāda Yoga tradition, where emotion is not suppressed but transformed through sound. The Nāda Yogi does not flee from sorrow; he listens to it. He places the drone of the *tanpura* beside his pain, not to escape it, but to bathe it in the frequency of presence. He does not analyse his fears; he chants to them, offering their tremour to the infinite pulse of Oṁ. In this way, the inner echoes become part of the excellent vibration, and what was once wound becomes wisdom.

This transformation is beautifully illustrated in the Śiva *Tāṇḍava Stotram*, composed by Rāvaṇa, the great devotee of Śiva. The verses vibrate with both fire and surrender, strength and supplication:

**"जटाटवीगलज्जलप्रवाहपावितस्थले
गलेऽवलम्ब्य लम्बितां भुजङ्गतुङ्गमालिकाम्।
डमड्डमड्डमड्डमन्निनादवड्डमर्वयं
चकार चण्डताण्डवं तनोतु नः शिवः शिवम्॥"**

Transliteration:

Jaṭāṭavī-gala-jjala-pravāha-pāvita-sthale
Gale'valambya lambitāṁ bhujaṅga-tuṅga-mālikām
Ḍamaḍ ḍamaḍ ḍamaḍ ḍamaṇ nināda-vaḍḍa-marvayaṁ
Cakāra caṇḍa-tāṇḍavaṁ tanotu naḥ śivaḥ śivam

Meaning:

"May Lord Śiva bless us with auspiciousness—He who dances His fierce Tāṇḍava, His matted locks dripping with Ganga's holy water, serpents adorning His neck, and the *ḍamaru's* wild rhythm reverberating through creation."

This hymn is not simply a devotional song; it is vibrational thunder. Every syllable is charged with movement and fire. Rāvaṇa, a being of immense ego, was transformed through this sound. His arrogance melted in the resonance of praise. Thus, the *Śiva Tāṇḍava Stotram* becomes an example of how sound transmutes emotion into devotion, resistance into reverence.

Modern neuroscience affirms what the sages knew. Sound engages the insula, a part of the brain responsible for self-awareness and empathy. It activates the anterior cingulate, tied to emotional regulation, and the nucleus accumbens, the seat of pleasure and reward. Chanting sacred syllables like Oṁ reduces activity in the default mode network—the neural pattern of constant mental chatter—and brings the practitioner into the present moment, the seat of stillness and clarity.

In this silence born of sound, the soul begins to remember, not as data or facts, but as a living vibration. It remembers the sacred sounds it once knew—the lullaby of the river, the hum of stars, the rhythm of breath in the womb. These are not metaphorical sounds. They are the actual language of the soul, and every *mantra*, every *stotra*, every whispered prayer is a way to bring them back into resonance.

Thus, sound, emotion, and memory form a sacred trinity within the seeker. When aligned, they become the most potent tools of awakening. When sound is heard not just through the ears but through the heart, emotion is no longer bondage—it becomes ***bhakti***, pure love. And memory is no longer past—it becomes ***smṛiti***, remembrance of the eternal.

In the soul's deepest chamber, beneath all thought, there is a single vibration—soft, steady, eternal. When all the world's sounds fall silent, that vibration remains. The saints have heard it, the *yogis* have sung it, and the seekers have wept in its echo. That vibration is the voice of the Self, calling us home.

Section 5: Sound and Enlightenment – The Silent Pulse beyond All Vibration

The journey of sound begins in the outer world, passes through the senses, reverberates through emotion and memory, and—if listened to with proper attention—ends in a place where there is no sound at all. This may seem paradoxical, but it is the deepest secret of spiritual realisation: sound, when pursued to its purest essence, dissolves into silence, and in that silence, the Self is revealed. It is not the absence of sound that matters, but the presence of awareness untouched by sound. This is the final stage of vibration—the stage where the knower, the knowing, and the known dissolve into one luminous field of being. This is enlightenment.

In the Vedantic tradition, sound is described in four progressive levels of refinement. This concept, articulated in the *Nātya Śāstra*, the *Tāntric Śaiva* texts, and echoed in the *Devī Purāṇa*, outlines the journey of speech—and hence, all vibration—from the unmanifest to the manifest:

- **Parā Vāk (परा वाक्)** – Supreme speech, existing in the causal body, undifferentiated, unborn, pure potential.
- **Paśyantī Vāk (पश्यन्ती वाक्)** – The intuitive form, seen within but not yet formed into language.
- **Madhyamā Vāk (मध्यमा वाक्)** – The subtle inner voice, mentally formed but not yet spoken.
- **Vaikharī Vāk (वैकरी वाक्)** – Gross, external speech; vibration expressed through the mouth.

Each level is subtler than the one below it. The spiritual path is one of reversing this descent—moving from the noise of Vaikharī back to the still source of Parā. It is not a rejection of sound, but a return to its origin. When the seeker no longer chases outer words but becomes quiet enough to hear Paśyantī, and still enough to feel Parā, they encounter the vibrationless vibration—the sound that does not move, the silence that speaks.

The *Maṇḍūkya Upaniṣad*, that exquisite scripture which offers the final wisdom on the sacred syllable Oṁ, leads us precisely to this threshold. After describing the three phonetic components of Oṁ—A, U, M—as symbolic of waking, dreaming, and deep sleep, it declares:

"अमात्रश्चतुर्थः। अव्यवहार्यं प्रपञ्चोपशमं शिवमद्वैतं चतुर्थं मन्यन्ते। स आत्मा स विज्ञेयः॥"

Amātraś caturthaḥ. Avyavahāryaṁ prapañcopaśamaṁ śivam advaitaṁ caturthaṁ manyante. Sa ātmā sa vijñeyaḥ.

(The fourth is that which has no measure, is beyond all transactions, the cessation of all phenomena, the peaceful, the blissful, the nondual. That is the Self; That is to be realized.)

Here, the *amātra*, the soundless part after the 'M' of Oṁ, is not emptiness but transcendence. It is the *śivaṁ*, the peaceful, which cannot be spoken, heard, or conceptualised. It is not an object of knowledge, but the subject of all knowing. It is the Self as awareness, shining alone, undisturbed by sound, thought, or world.

This silence is not the negation of sound, but its consummation. In the stillness that follows the final syllable, the seeker does not fall into the void but enters the source of being. The sound does not disappear; it fulfils its purpose—to guide the mind back to its origin. This is why *mantra japa*, the repetition of sacred sound, is so central in all spiritual traditions—not as superstition, but as a method of deconstructing the ego through vibration. The mantra vibrates within until the mind itself begins to mirror its rhythm, and when the mind becomes steady, the *mantra* drops away, and only being remains.

This truth is celebrated in the *Dakṣiṇāmūrti Stotra*, attributed to Śaṅkarācārya. It honours Śiva as the silent guru who teaches through mere presence:

**"मौनव्याख्या प्रकटित परब्रह्मतत्त्वं युवानं
वर्षिष्ठान्ते वसदृषिगणैरावृतं ब्रह्मनिष्ठैः।
आचार्येन्द्रं करकलित चिन्मुद्रमानन्दमूर्तिं
स्वात्मारामं मुदितवदनं दक्षिणामूर्तिमीडे॥"**

Transliteration:
Maunavyākhyā prakaṭita parabrahmatattvaṁ yuvānaṁ
Varṣiṣṭhānte vasadṛṣigaṇairāvṛtaṁ brahmaniṣṭhaiḥ
Ācāryendraṁ karakalita cinmudramānandamūrtiṁ
Svātmārāmaṁ muditavadanaṁ dakṣiṇāmūrtimīḍe
Meaning:
"I worship Dakṣiṇāmūrti, the young teacher seated among wise sages, whose mere silence reveals the highest truth of Brahman, who expresses knowledge through the gesture of consciousness, who dwells in his Self, and whose face is radiant with joy."

Here, the teaching is not given through words or sound, but through *mauna*, the power of silence. Dakṣiṇāmūrti does not chant; He vibrates. He does not speak; He radiates. He is the living embodiment of Parā Vāk, the silent root of all speech. This is the ideal of the spiritual journey: to move from expression to essence, from sound to source.

In yogic meditation, when the seeker enters deep states of absorption, they may begin to hear the inner nāda—a subtle hum, a high-pitched ring, a low drumbeat within the body. These sounds are not imaginary; they are real vibrations in the subtle body, heard when the grosser inputs of the senses are stilled. Ancient *yogis* identified ten such inner sounds, corresponding to stages of internal awakening. Yet even these are to be transcended. The final goal is not to dwell in the sound, but to cross beyond it, into the anāhata—the unstruck, unoriginated vibration which is silence vibrating as light.

In the final stages of awakening, the seeker no longer hears sound as an external thing; they hear it as the Self. Every sound is recognised as arising in consciousness, resting in consciousness, and dissolving back into it. This is the state of the *jīvanmukta*, the liberated while living, who walks through the world as if it were a song they no longer need to understand, for they have become the silence between the notes.

The *Śiva Purāṇa* summarises this transcendental teaching beautifully:
"शब्दो जायते तस्मात् तस्मिन्शब्दो लयं ययाति।
शिवो हि शब्दमूलः, शब्दस्य च शिवः परम्॥"

Transliteration:
Śabdo jāyate tasmāt tasmin śabdo layaṁ yayāti
Śivo hi śabdamūlaḥ, śabdasya ca śivaḥ param
Meaning:
"From Him arises sound, and into Him sound dissolves. Śiva is the root of sound, and also the final destination of all sound."

In this vision, sound is the path, and Śiva is the goal. The seeker who chants, who listens, who meditates on vibration, is not worshipping a god outside himself. He is awakening the Śiva within, who pulses not with noise, but with stillness more profound than silence.

In this stillness, all sound is present, yet no sound is necessary.

And thus, the journey of sound is complete.

Chapter 5

Sight – Seeing Beyond the Visible

Section 1: The Light That Sees – Vision as the Gateway to Inner Illumination

Before there was colour, there was light. Before there was an image, there was awareness. Sight—the most celebrated of human senses—is often mistaken as a mere mechanical process of receiving photons and interpreting patterns. But to those who peer deeper, to the sages, seers, and awakened souls, sight is not only a way of perceiving the world; it is a doorway to the soul. To see rightly is not to see more things—it is to see through them, beyond them, and finally, within them. In the realm of spiritual experience, the eyes do not simply observe reality—they reveal it.

The journey of visual perception begins long before the world appears. According to Vedic cosmology, vision is rooted in the element of Agni (अग्नि), fire. Agni is not just the fire in the hearth or the blaze in the sky; it is the subtle light that makes perception possible. The Taittirīya Upaniṣad declares:

"तस्माद्वै एतस्मादात्मन आकाशः सम्भूतः । आकाशाद्वायुः । वायोरग्निः ।"

Tasmād vai eṭasmād ātmana ākāśaḥ sambhūtaḥ | Ākāśād vāyuḥ | Vāyor agniḥ.

(From that very Self arose space; from space, air; from air, fire.)

This fire—Agni—is the principle of transformation, of illumination, of discernment. In the gross body, Agni becomes the eyes, the light of perception. In the subtle body, Agni becomes clarity, vision, and insight. Sight, therefore, is not the reception of outer forms but the play of fire and consciousness—the meeting of inner light and outer light.

The *Bhagavad Gītā*, in its eleventh chapter, gives us one of the most awe-inspiring descriptions of divine sight. When Arjuna, overwhelmed and lost, asks Krishna to reveal his universal form, Krishna says:

"दिव्यं ददामि ते चक्षुः पश्य मे योगमैश्वरम् ।"

Divyaṁ dadāmi te cakṣuḥ paśya me yogam aiśvaram.

(I grant you divine sight; behold My cosmic yoga.)

What follows is not a new world entering Arjuna's eyes, but a new capacity of vision given to him—a divine upgrade to his perception. This sight pierces the veil of appearances and beholds reality as it is. The *Gītā* teaches us that true vision is not about improving the eyes, but about purifying the seer.

In the physiological body, vision begins when light enters the eye, passing through the cornea, aqueous humour, lens, and vitreous body, finally reaching the retina, where specialised photoreceptors—rods and cones—translate photons into neural impulses. But what happens next is even more extraordinary. These impulses travel via the optic nerve to the lateral geniculate nucleus of the thalamus, and then to the primary visual cortex in the occipital lobe. Yet the experience of seeing does not occur in the eye or the cortex—it occurs in the field of consciousness. The brain processes images, but it is the Self that sees.

Neuroscience tells us that visual processing is predictive. The brain fills in gaps, anticipates patterns, edits, and reconstructs visual data based on memory, bias, emotion, and learning. But spiritual traditions have long known this truth: we do not see what is—we see what we are prepared to see. The *ṛṣis* of old recognised that to see clearly, one must not only open the eyes but also purify the mind.

This is echoed in the *Kena Upaniṣad*, which asks:

"चक्षुषो चक्षुरिति ।"

Cakṣuṣo cakṣur iti.

(It is the Eye of the eye.)

That which gives power to the eyes to see is not the eye itself, but a deeper light—the light of pure awareness, which illumines all perception. The eyes are instruments, but the Self is the seer. To forget this is to remain bound to the surface. To realise this is to begin the awakening process.

In the yogic tradition, the third eye (*ājñā cakra*) is not a metaphor. It is a subtle organ of perception located between the eyebrows, said to be the seat of intuition and higher vision. When activated through meditation, breath, and mantra, the third eye reveals not the world outside, but the truth within. It sees not form, but essence; not motion, but stillness. This is the vision that saints speak of, where the outer world fades, and the inner world becomes radiant with insight.

When we speak of sight as a gateway to enlightenment, we are not speaking of physical sight alone. We are speaking of the shift from looking to seeing, from seeing to knowing, and from knowing to being. The path begins with light, moves through image, and ends in presence.

As the great Śaiva sage Abhinavagupta wrote:

"यदृच्छया दृश्यते विश्वं तदृच्छया न दृश्यते।

Yadṛcchayā dṛśyate viśvaṁ tadṛcchayā na dṛśyate.

(That by which the universe is seen cannot itself be seen by the same means.)

To behold the world is a gift. But to behold the one who beholds the world—that is liberation.

And so, sight, when rightly understood, is not an obstacle to truth but its revelation. Every image, every beam of light, every shadow cast on the wall of perception is an invitation to look deeper, not with the eyes, but with the soul's vision. The world dazzles the eye, but only silence reveals the seer.

This is the light that does not flicker, the seeing that does not grasp, the eye that does not blink. It is the vision of the Real.

Section 2: The Structure of Seeing – The Eyes, the Brain, and the Light of Consciousness

If the eyes are the lamps of the body, then what they illuminate is far more than physical form. The human eye, that orb of moist clarity and intricate layering, is more than a biological camera. It is a miraculous fusion of evolutionary precision and divine architecture. But to see it only as an organ is to miss its essence. It is through the eye that the outer world enters us, and through which the inner world begins to reflect outward. In Indian metaphysics, this delicate interplay is not passive observation but *darśana*—the act of sacred seeing.

The anatomical eye is composed of multiple layers, each of which reflects not only biological function but also spiritual symbolism. The transparent cornea, like the threshold of perception, allows the sacred light of the world to enter while bending it just enough to prepare it for transformation. It is not unlike the subtle mind, which must allow impressions in without distortion. The aqueous humour, constantly flowing, maintains the pressure and purity within the anterior chamber, mirroring the subtle flow of awareness that must remain clean and undisturbed for correct perception to arise. The iris, the coloured ring unique in every being, is nature's fingerprint upon the eye—it expands and contracts not merely mechanically but poetically, regulating how much light the soul is ready to receive. It acts with the reverence of a priest, tending to the flame of the sacred fire within the temple, adjusting the flame not to destroy or dazzle, but to nourish the seeker's inner gaze. The pupil, dark and deep, is far more than an aperture—it is a void of potent mystery. Into it pours the world's light, yet it appears black, unlit. It reminds us of the profound *Upanishadic* truth that within darkness, *vidyā*—the highest knowledge—is concealed. It is the place where form disappears and awareness begins—an opening not just into the eye, but into the infinite stillness of the Self.

The lens of the eye, suspended by delicate ciliary muscles, focuses light upon the retina, which is not merely a screen, but a living field of photoreceptors—rods attuned to the grey mystery of night, cones gifted with the spectrum of colours that clothe the world. These cells translate light into neural signals, launching them onto the optic nerve—the pathway of vision, which carries more than just information. It carries meaning, attention, and presence.

As the signals travel along this optic highway, they do not immediately move into vision. First, they reach the optic chiasm, where the left and right visual fields cross—a symbolic reflection that seeing always involves integration, a union of opposites. From there, the signals are processed by the lateral geniculate nucleus (LGN), where sorting, comparison, and initial refinement occur. Finally, they reach the primary visual cortex in the occipital lobe, the backmost chamber of the brain, where vision becomes recognition.

But what is it that truly sees? Does the brain see? Do neurons comprehend? Can electricity become experience? The sages have long insisted otherwise. The Kena Upaniṣad again answers:

"यन्मनसा न मनुते येनाहुर् मनो मतम्। तद् एव ब्रह्म त्वं विद्धि नेदं यद् इदं उपासते॥"

Yanmanasā na manute yenāhurmano matam | Tad eva brahma tvaṁ viddhi nedaṁ yad idaṁ upāsate ||

(That which the mind does not think, but by which the mind thinks—know That to be Brahman, not what people worship here.)

This shloka also applies to vision. The brain interprets, but awareness illumines. The act of seeing is completed not by the physical or even the mental, but by the conscious witness—the Self. We may possess healthy eyes and a sound brain, yet remain blind to the truth. Conversely, the blind sage may see the subtle form of reality with an eye untouched by biology.

In *Yoga* and *Tantra*, it is said that the *ājñā cakra*, located between the eyebrows, corresponds not only to intuition but also to the optic system. The pineal gland, nestled deep within the brain, is often referred to as the "third eye," not without reason. Although it no longer receives direct light, it remains sensitive to the rhythms of light and dark, thereby governing circadian cycles. More symbolically, it is the seat of inner illumination, perceiving what the outer eyes cannot.

Abhinavagupta, the philosopher-mystic of Kashmir Śaivism, wrote of *vimarśa*, the reflective awareness that turns inward upon itself. Sight is *prakaśa*—the light. But without *vimarśa*—self-reflective seeing—it is incomplete. The eye sees, but only when awareness sees itself seeing does actual knowledge arise.

To understand this, the Śiva Sūtras say:

"चित्तं मन्त्रः।"

Cittaṁ mantraḥ.

(Consciousness itself is a mantra.)

And a mantra is nothing but a vibration turned into awareness. In the same way, sight is light turned to meaning, and meaning turned to being.

The human eye is nothing but a window. The retina is nothing but a screen. The real image is seen not in the brain, but in the space between the seen and the seer. To awaken that space is to begin to see not merely with the eyes, but with wisdom.

Section 3: Inner Vision and the Third Eye – Awakening the Power of Direct Seeing

The eye opens not once in life, but twice. The first is when the newborn child is exposed to the brilliance of external light, gasping into the world of form. The second, subtler awakening happens later—perhaps after years, lifetimes, or in a moment of grace—when the inner eye opens and beholds not objects, but the source of seeing itself. This inner eye, called the third eye, is not a poetic metaphor. It is the nucleus of inner vision, known across mystical, yogic, and scriptural traditions as the *ājñā cakra* (आज्ञा चक्र)—the command centre of insight, intuition, and direct knowing.

According to Yogic anatomy, the human being is not merely a physical body but a layered being composed of multiple sheaths (*kośas*) and subtle channels (*nāḍīs*) that carry *prāṇa*, the vital energy. Along the *suṣumnā nāḍī*, the central energy channel running parallel to the spine, lie seven major cakras, or energy centres. Of these, the sixth, located between the eyebrows, is known as the *ājñā cakra.* Derived from the root "*ājñā*," meaning "command" or "authority", this centre is described as the seat of divine will, discrimination, and wisdom.

Scriptures such as the *Ṣaṭcakra Nirūpaṇa* describe the *ājñā cakra* as a two-petaled lotus, its duality symbolising the convergence of opposites—sun and moon, *ida* and *piṅgalā*, mind and intellect. In this union, the seeker gains access not only to symbolic sight but to direct perception beyond the senses.

"इयं मनोमयी विद्या नित्या ब्रह्मस्वरूपिणी।
ब्रह्मादिस्थावरान्तान्तं जगत् व्याप्य स्थितासदा॥"

— *Ṣaṭcakra Nirūpaṇa, verse 35*

This Vidyā (inner light) is of the nature of mind, eternal, the very form of Brahman. Pervading all from Brahmā down to the smallest creature, she dwells as the ever-present awareness.

Physiologically, this cakra aligns approximately with the epithalamic structures of the brain, particularly the pineal gland, often referred to in mystical traditions as the "seat of the soul." French philosopher René Descartes described the pineal gland as the point where the immaterial soul interacts with the material body—a view echoed in Indian texts that describe this organ as the bridge between prākṛti (nature) and puruṣa (consciousness).

Although modern science remains cautious in affirming metaphysical claims, a growing body of research suggests that the pineal gland plays a significant role in regulating circadian rhythms by producing melatonin. This hormone governs the body's sleep-wake cycles. In their 1995 publication in Neuroscience & Biobehavioral Reviews, Reiter and Tan outlined the sensitivity of the pineal gland to light and its unique role in translating photic signals into endocrine responses, suggesting that it may hold deeper ties to our neuroconscious interface than previously understood.

Moreover, the retinal and pineal pathways are phylogenetically linked—that is, they share a common evolutionary ancestry. As researcher David Klein of the National Institute of Child Health and Human Development points out, the pineal gland can be considered a "light-sensitive structure", not in the direct optical sense, but through its profound receptivity to electromagnetic rhythms. In yogic symbolism, this subtle light perception becomes jñāna dṛiṣṭi (ज्ञान दृष्टि)—the inner vision that knows without seeing.

But why does ancient Indian philosophy so emphatically speak of a third eye? And what does it truly see?

In Śaiva Tantra, the third eye is not merely a mystical spot; it is the source of direct knowledge, prajñā (प्रज्ञा)—that which transcends memory, deduction, or inference. Lord Śiva, the master of Yogīs, is often depicted with a flaming third eye at the centre of His forehead. It is not an ornament; it is a cosmic fire of perception. This eye does not see the world—it burns through illusion.

The Liṅga Purāṇa tells us:

"त्रिनेत्रं त्रिगुणातीतं त्रिलोकेशं त्रिलोचनम्।
स्वयं ज्योतिर्निजाकारं नित्यं योगिनमाश्रयम्॥"

He with three eyes, beyond the three guṇas, the Lord of the three worlds, the Three-Eyed One, is self-luminous, whose form is eternal, the refuge of yogīs.

This eye is the destroyer of ***māyā***, the veil of illusion that keeps beings bound to the ever-shifting drama of name and form. When Śiva opens his third eye, time collapses, karma is incinerated, and **pure awareness remains**. The same truth applies to the *sādhaka* (spiritual aspirant). When the third eye opens—not literally, but as a shift in consciousness, the seeker no longer needs belief or scripture. Truth becomes directly visible.

In psychological terms, this can be seen as the transition from sensory cognition to intuitive insight. The psychologist Carl Jung, working within a Western framework, understood this dimension well. In his lectures on *Kundalini Yoga*, Jung stated that the awakening of the *ājñā* centre corresponded to the integration of the unconscious mind into conscious awareness — a harmonising of opposites that produces vision without projection. This, he suggested, was the true beginning of individuation—the birth of the fully aware Self.

However, such a vision is not simply mystical; it has practical implications. In a 2014 paper published in *Frontiers in Psychology*, neuroscientists Jared D. Freeman and Arturo Mannino investigated how focused meditative attention leads to activation in the default mode network (DMN), particularly in regions associated with meta-awareness—the awareness of awareness itself. This aligns with what the *Yogis* have always taught: when the gaze turns inward and rests steadily on the *ājñā cakra*, the practitioner begins to observe thought without identification. The seer is disentangled from the seen.

Meditative disciplines such as *trāṭaka*—the yogic practice of fixed gazing on a candle flame—are designed to train this very capacity. Over time, the practitioner closes their eyes, yet the flame persists—not as an afterimage, but as an inner light. This is not imagination. This is *pratyakṣa* (प्रत्यक्ष)—direct vision of the subtle. The *Gheraṇḍa Saṁhitā* prescribes *trāṭaka* not merely for ocular strength, but for awakening the divine **eye**.

"त्राटकं तु समाचारेत् सुषुम्णा-विवरे स्थिरः।
यत्र दृष्टिर्लयं याति तत्र मनो विलीयते॥"

— *Gheraṇḍa Saṁhitā 1.53*

When one practices trāṭaka on the subtle inner channel (suṣumnā), where the gaze dissolves, the mind also merges.

This dissolution is not emptiness. It is clarity beyond thought. When the mind stops generating images, the third eye sees what has always been present: stillness, presence, and truth. It is this state that the *ṛṣis* called *turiya*—the fourth, beyond waking, dreaming, and deep sleep. It is the vision not of things, but of being itself.

In this sense, the third eye is not an addition, but a return. It is not a new organ, but the awakening of the witness. It is the subtle recognition that all seeing occurs in consciousness, and that consciousness itself is never seen. The Chandogya Upaniṣad hints at this:

"तदेति तन्मन्यतेऽहमिति। सोऽहमस्मि।"

(Tadeti tan manyate aham iti. So'ham asmi.)
(That which knows "I am that"—verily, I am that.)

Thus, when the third eye opens, the distinction between "seer" and "seen" collapses. The world is no longer out there, but within the field of awareness. What the physical eyes show as form, the inner eye reveals as presence.

Modern researchers exploring consciousness and non-duality, such as Dr. Andrew Newberg and Robert K.C. Forman, have noted that advanced meditators consistently describe a phase of awareness that is contentless, luminous, and intensely present. In Newberg's neuroimaging studies of Tibetan monks and Indian *yogis*, bursts of activity were detected in the parietal lobes and anterior cingulate, regions associated with selfless awareness and focused attention. These findings suggest that what ancient texts described as *śānta dṛṣṭi* (शान्त दृष्टि)—a peaceful, liberated vision—is not only authentic but also neurologically supported.

Ultimately, the third eye does not make one clairvoyant in the popular sense. It removes the veil, not by adding supernatural perception, but by dissolving the need for perception. When one sees truly, there is nothing to seek. The world no longer appears as fragmented, but as a single, continuous, and conscious flow. This is *darśana* in its highest form—not merely seeing the deity in a shrine, but seeing the divine in all things.

As the *Śiva Sūtras* say:

"ज्ञानाṁ जाग्रत्।"

Jñānaṁ jāgrat.

(True knowledge is awakening.)

Awakening comes not through the eyes, but through the opening of inner vision. In the silence behind thought, the light behind form, the presence behind identity—that is where the third eye waits. It does not demand ritual or religion; the only thing it requires is readiness.

When it opens, it does not show you another world. It shows you this world as it truly is—timeless, whole, sacred.

Section 4: Symbol, Vision, and the Sacred Image – The Eye in Myth and Temple

The eye has never been just an organ. Long before it was examined under microscopes or mapped through neuroimaging, it was revered as a symbol, etched into stone, woven into scripture, painted upon the brows of deities and guardians alike. In ancient India, the eye was not merely seen as the window of the soul—it was the soul looking outward, bearing witness to a world that was both sacred and impermanent. From the mystical hymns of the Vedas to the dark sanctums of South Indian temples, the symbol of the eye has remained a central axis around which the human and the divine rotate. It is the icon through which vision becomes veneration.

The Vedic seers, or *ṛṣis*, often equated the Sun (सूर्य) with the divine eye that illumines the cosmos. In the Ṛgveda, one of the earliest and most profound declarations of this is found:

"चक्षुर्देवः आयनाय नमः।"

Cakṣur devaḥ āyanāya namaḥ

(To the divine eye, the pathway of light, I offer my salutations.)

Here, the Sun is not just a celestial body—it is the eye of Varuṇa, the seer of all actions, the eternal witness. In Ṛgveda 1.50.10, Sūrya is addressed as:

"तच्चक्षुरेभ्यः प्रतिष्ठं मनोजवम्।"

(That eye, swift as the mind, established for the seeing of beings.)

The symbol of the eye is thus not inert; it is movement, cognition, illumination. It watches not from without, but from within creation, pervading both the knower and the known. The eye is the Sun, and the Sun is awareness itself.

In Indian temple architecture, this idea finds visible expression in the form of the *netra* (नेत्र)—the sacred eye carved onto idols and temple walls, often large, radiant, and open, inviting *darśana* (the sacred act of seeing and being seen). Every deity has eyes that do not look passively—they penetrate. They are not fixed to a direction—they see through the veils of matter into the aspirant's soul.

In the ancient Śrī Vidyā tradition, the goddess Lalitā Tripurasundarī is often meditated upon as possessing three eyes, symbolising *icchā* (will), *jñāna* (knowledge), and *kriyā* (action). The third eye in this context is not ornamental—it is the axis of transcendent awareness, from which flows unobstructed compassion and insight. The Lalitā Sahasranāma describes her as:

"त्रिनयना ललिता"

Trinayanā Lalitā

(She who has three eyes, the beautiful one.)

The three eyes signify the *trikāla dṛiṣṭi*—the capacity to perceive the past, present, and future—not as time-bound states, but as simultaneous realities within consciousness. Her third eye is the symbol of timeless perception.

In temples, especially those dedicated to Śiva and Devi, the *netronmīlana* (opening of the eyes) is a sacred ritual performed during *prāṇa pratiṣṭhā*, when the life force is invoked into a *mūrti* (idol). Until the eyes are opened—often with a ritualistic stroke of a chisel or brush—the idol remains a form. After the *netra* is opened, it becomes *sākṣāt darśana*, a living embodiment of the divine. The eye is not merely painted—it is awakened. The icon does not look—it sees.

In the *Nāṭyaśāstra*, Bharata describes how, in classical dance, eye movements (*dṛiṣṭi bhedas*) convey spiritual and emotional intention. They are not just aesthetic but psycho-spiritual gestures. The dancer's eye becomes a transmitter of *rasa* (aesthetic emotion), conveying not only mood but states of transcendental perception. Thus, even in human performance, the eye becomes a bridge between *bhāva* (feeling) and *rasa* (divine flavour).

Let us also consider the iconic representation of Śiva as Natarāja, the Lord of Dance. While the dance itself encodes the cycle of creation and destruction, His third eye stands at the heart of this symbolism. When Śiva opened His third eye to annihilate Kāmadeva, the god of desire, He did not destroy out of violence, but to burn illusion, allowing the *yogi* to see without craving and to love without grasping. The fire that emerged was not wrath—it was *tapas*, the purifying flame of insight. As described in the *Śiva Purāṇa*:

"त्रिनेत्रं ज्वलनं शान्तं योगिनां ध्यानगोचरम्।"

(Three-eyed, blazing and serene, He is accessible only through the inner meditation of yogis.)

Temple sculpture often emphasises this symbolism. In the great temples of Khajurāho, Madurai, Chidambaram, and Ellora, one sees divine figures not only adorned with multiple eyes, but with faces bearing gazes that seem to look inward and outward simultaneously. This dual gaze—*antarmukha* and *bahirmukha*—is the heart of all spiritual seeing. The outer eye searches, while the inner eye knows.

Even the sacred diagrams (*yantras*) used in Tantric rituals reflect this vision. The Bindu, the central point of the *Śrī Yantra*, is often referred to as the divine eye of awareness, from which all vision originates. It is the *śūnya*, the void that sees all, yet remains unseen. In esoteric commentaries such as the *Bhāvanopaniṣad*, it is written:

"बिन्दुरूपिणी शक्तिः सर्वदर्शिनी हि या।"

(She who is in the form of the Bindu, the one who sees all.)

And so, the eye becomes the *bindu* and the *bhāva*, the point and the emotion, the icon and the insight. Whether carved in granite, reflected in bronze, or painted in saffron pigment on a village shrine, the eye is never static. It is always waiting to be met by the soul that dares to look back.

In this meeting, between the gaze of the deity and the gaze of the devotee, *darśana* happens. However, *darśana* is not one-directional; it is not merely seeing God, but God seeing it. The temple, then, is not a hall of worship—it is a theatre of seeing, where self-consciousness is dissolved into divine presence.

As scholar Diana Eck notes in *Darśan: Seeing the Divine Image in India*, "*Darśan* is more than seeing, it is being in the presence of the divine, of allowing oneself to be seen in return. It is not passive reception; it is participatory vision." In this way, sight itself becomes an offering, a surrender, a merging.

And what does the soul see when it sees rightly? Not form, but flame. Not features, but presence. Not object, but essence. This is why the symbol of the eye is never truly closed. It is always watching—not to judge, but to remember, to remind the aspirant that the divine is not far, not hidden, not beyond; rather, it is looking back through their very eyes.

In the end, the sacred eye is not outside us; it is the mirror of the self, quietly waiting behind the forehead, waiting behind the heart, reflecting not what is, but what always was.

Section 5: The Eye of Non-duality – Seeing the World as One Light

There comes a point on the spiritual path when the world does not change, yet everything appears transformed. The trees still sway in the wind, rivers still flow, faces still age, and shadows still fall. But to the awakened eye, these appearances no longer conceal the truth—they reveal it. This is the shift from duality to non-duality. It is not a belief or a philosophy alone; it is a direct alteration in the quality of perception. One no longer sees "self" and "other," "here" and "there," "seer" and "seen"—but a continuous field of being those pulses as one conscious light.

The acquisition of new information does not mark the journey from duality to non-duality, but by the dissolution of false perception. It begins subtly, when the seeker begins to notice that every act of seeing is also an act of separation. The eyes, trained to distinguish between light and dark, beauty and flaw, pleasure and pain, construct a world of categories. This is the world of *nāma-rūpa*, of name and form. At the surface level, the dualistic mind assumes that there is a subject inside the body looking out at an external object. The 'I' sees the 'world.' But as meditation deepens and the inner faculties begin to quiet, this structure begins to tremble. The distance between seer and seen shrinks. Eventually, what remains is only seeing—no seer, no seen. This is the eye of non-duality.

Non-dual perception is not an esoteric abstraction; it is a felt experience, often arising spontaneously in moments of deep stillness. A person may sit before a mountain, a candle, or even a blank wall—and suddenly, the boundaries dissolve. The gaze is no longer moving outward toward something. Instead, it rests in itself. What is seen is not different from the seeing. Awareness and its object collapse into oneness. But how does one reach this space? Not through force, not through endless thinking. The process is one of clarifying vision, much like cleaning the lens of a camera. The dirt on the lens—made of mental agitation, emotional conditioning, spiritual pride, and habitual thought—is not removed by grasping at insight. It is dissolved through stilling, observing, and, most importantly, through grace. In nearly all spiritual traditions of the East, it is emphasised that one cannot simply "think" oneself into non-duality. The mind, which is itself the instrument of duality, cannot produce the non-dual. This is where the role of the *Guru* becomes indispensable. The *Guru* is not merely a teacher or a source of information. The *Guru* is the embodiment of the non-dual state—one whose very presence radiates the silent unity that the seeker longs to find. To see the world as one light, the aspirant must be initiated into that vision, and this is done not through academic instruction but through a subtle transmission of energy, presence, and understanding. The *Guru* is the mirror in which the disciple finally sees not the *Guru's* face, but their true face—formless, luminous, and free.

This transition from duality to non-duality often begins with trust. The seeker, bound by fear and separation, cannot leap directly into oneness. However, through the relationship with the *Guru*, a bridge is formed. The disciple begins to feel that they are not alone in their mind; there is a presence, a guiding eye that sees with them, and through them. Gradually, the vision that once pointed outward toward multiplicity turns inward toward unity.

This is why in many traditions, the disciple is instructed to fix the gaze between the eyebrows, to meditate upon the space of inner light, and to surrender the fruits of vision to the feet of the *Guru.* The feet, in this symbolism, are not simply anatomical—they are the lowest part of the highest truth, the place where divinity touches the earth. Through surrender, the seeker's vision is lowered from the pride of seeing "things" to the humility of seeing truth. Non-dual sight is not about seeing more. It is about seeing less and being more. It is the end of projection, interpretation, and grasping. The world no longer needs to be understood—it needs only to be seen as it is.

When these seen dawns arrive, it does not remove the world—it transfigures it. The face of a stranger becomes your own, the dying leaf on the branch glows with the same aliveness as your beating heart, the walls no longer confine you—they melt, the eyes are open, but there is no tension behind them. Vision becomes a resting, not an effort. It is not detachment; it is intimacy with everything.

This intimacy is the hallmark of the non-dual eye. Where the dualistic mind seeks knowledge, the non-dual heart knows presence. Where the dualistic eye looks outward to conquer, the non-dual gaze returns inward to recognise. You do not merge with the world—you discover you were never apart.

And in that final realisation, there is no thunder, no announcement. The shift is gentle, unassuming — a flower blooms, a breath softens, and a silent joy rises for no reason. And you know—not because you have seen, but because you are seeing—that the light that shines in your eye, in the sun, and in every soul is the same.

This is the Eye of Non-duality.

Chapter 6

Smell – The Memory of Spirit

Section 1: Fragrance and the Forgotten – Smell as the Thread of Soul Memory

Among the senses, smell is the most ancient and often the most underestimated. It lacks the immediacy of sight, the directionality of sound, or the complexity of touch. Yet within its apparent subtlety lies a mysterious power: the ability to call the soul back to itself. Smell is intimate, interior, and instinctual—it does not merely perceive the world, it remembers it. A single breath of fragrance can awaken a memory buried for decades. A scent can collapse time, dissolve barriers, and invoke a presence far deeper than thought. For the sages of old, smell was not only about the outer world—it was a pathway to spirit, a channel of ancestral memory, and the very fragrance of consciousness itself.

Physiologically, smell is the only sense that bypasses the thalamus—the brain's relay centre—and travels directly to the limbic system, the seat of emotion and long-term memory. This unique neural route allows olfactory input to influence emotional states immediately, bypassing rational filters. The olfactory receptor neurons, located in the olfactory epithelium high inside the nasal cavity, are capable of detecting even the faintest molecular traces. These neurons send signals directly to the olfactory bulb, which is intimately connected to the amygdala and hippocampus—centres responsible for emotional response and episodic memory, respectively. This is why the smell of burning incense can evoke memories of a childhood temple, the scent of rain can summon a lost love, and the aroma of sandalwood can plunge a *yogi* into a trance.

This biological intimacy is mirrored in spiritual literature. The Ṛgveda, in its hymns to Agni, repeatedly speaks of fragrance, not merely as a sensory delight but as evidence of the divine. Agni is not only fire; he is the carrier of offerings, and the rising fragrance of oblations is his language with the gods. Smell, in this view, is not human—it is celestial. The rising smoke, carrying the scent of ghee and soma, becomes a bridge between earth and heaven, between mortal and immortal.

"यज्ञेन यज्ञमयजन्त देवास्तानि धर्माणि प्रथमान्यासन्।"

(Through sacrifice, the gods performed sacrifice. These were the first sacred acts.)

The fragrant fire of *yajña* is not an act of burning—it is an act of communion. The scent that rises is not lost—it reaches the unseen.

In the *Upaniṣads*, smell is associated with *prāṇa*, the life-force. The Chāndogya Upaniṣad describes smell as residing in the earth, and the earth itself as the embodied smell of consciousness. The teaching is clear: what we smell is not merely substance but the *samskāra* (impression) it carries. A flower has not only petals but memory. A body has not only skin but also a spirit. The scent is the trace of the Self clothed in form.

Modern psychology echoes these insights. In a seminal 2004 paper published in *Science*, researchers Herz and Engen explored how odour-evoked memories are more emotionally potent and vivid than memories associated with any other sense. Their findings revealed that olfaction is uniquely tied to autobiographical recall, suggesting that scent plays a key role in identity continuity. In mystical terms, this means smell is not peripheral—it is the signature of the soul in time.

The role of smell in sacred rituals reinforces this intuition. Every temple, from the modest home shrine to the towering *garbhagṛhas* of South India, is suffused with fragrance: the burning of camphor, the wafting of incense, the anointing with rosewater, sandalwood paste, and jasmine oil. These are not mere embellishments—they are vibrational technologies. Each scent has its own frequency, mood, and vibration. Smell is used to cleanse the subtle body, to invoke deities, to awaken devotion. In *tantric* practice, certain *gandha-tattvas* (fragrance elements) are employed to activate specific *cakras*, awaken *kuṇḍalinī*, and dissolve egoic structure. The smell becomes a mantra without sound—a signal to the inner being that the sacred is near.

The Śaiva and Śākta traditions, in particular, place deep emphasis on the olfactory dimension of worship. In the Saundarya Laharī, attributed to Śrī Śaṅkarācārya, it is said that the mere scent of the Goddess's body causes divine intoxication, sending sages into ecstatic silence. Here, smell is not passive—it is transformative. It is not experienced—it is absorbed, like *prāṇa*. The smell of Divinity is not an object—it is a state.

In esoteric literature, smell is also linked with ancestral presence. Many spiritual practitioners report the sudden appearance of specific fragrances—such as musk, sandal, and attar—during deep meditation or spiritual events. These are understood not as hallucinations but as signatures of presence—the astral trace of beings, human or divine. In this view, scent is the language of spirit, and to smell is to be attuned to the memory field of existence.

Even death carries its scent—not only biologically, but spiritually. Ancient seers described that at the moment of a great saint's leaving the body, a profound fragrance often pervades the air. It is said that this final offering of the body is a release of all its karmic impressions, sublimated into fragrance. The body leaves, but its spirit lingers as scent.

Thus, smell is not just a sense. It is a sacred thread, connecting body to soul, matter to memory, time to eternity. It is the Subtlest of the gross, the Grossest of the subtle. It moves beneath thought, beneath emotion, beneath even awareness, touching a space we do not name, yet know intimately.

To awaken this sense is not merely to enjoy aromas but to become sensitive to the traces of spirit. It is to understand that everything we encounter carries a scent—not only objects, but thoughts, emotions, people, and places. To smell rightly is to remember rightly. It is to return to the first breath that knew the world not as separate, but as scented with sacredness.

Section 2: The Breath of Knowing – The Physiology of Smell and the Spirit Within

Smell enters not through conscious decision but through the breath, softly, continuously, and often unnoticed. We may close our eyes, still our tongue, fold our hands, but as long as we breathe, we are smelling. It is the most persistent of the senses and, paradoxically, the most silent. We do not hear scent, we do not touch it, we do not see it. Yet it enters, imprints, and influences us in the most intimate ways. And it does this through a pathway that is among the oldest in human evolution, both biologically and spiritually.

At the front of the human nasal cavity, in a patch of tissue smaller than a postage stamp, lies the olfactory epithelium. Embedded within it are millions of olfactory receptor neurons, each equipped with cilia—microscopic hairs that interact with airborne chemical molecules. These molecules, whether from rose, earth, sweat, or sandalwood, dissolve in the mucus of the nasal cavity and bind to these receptors. The result is a chain of biochemical reactions that generate an electrical impulse. This impulse travels along the olfactory nerve (cranial nerve I) to the olfactory bulb, a structure situated just above the nasal cavity and just beneath the frontal cortex of the brain.

Unlike other senses, olfactory signals do not pass through the thalamus, the brain's central relay station. Instead, smell takes a direct path to the amygdala and the hippocampus—the emotional and memory centres of the brain. This direct route explains why smell can instantly trigger memories, feelings, or subconscious associations without any conscious processing. A fragrance bypasses cognition—it goes straight to the core of the self.

This physiological intimacy aligns precisely with the understanding of the ancient sages. In yogic physiology, the nose is associated with *prāṇa vāyu,* the life-breath that governs inhalation and upward movement of energy. It is said that what we inhale, we become. The breath is not just air—it is charged with impressions, subtle memories, karmic threads, and unseen energies. Every smell we encounter shapes our inner atmosphere, whether we are aware of it or not.

In the endocrine system, this connection becomes even more profound. The hypothalamus, which receives olfactory input, is also the regulatory command centre for the body's hormonal secretions. From hunger and thirst to sexual desire and fear, the hypothalamus governs how we feel and behave. The scents we inhale profoundly influence this system. For example, pheromones—odourless chemical messengers—are detected through a secondary olfactory system called the vomeronasal organ (VNO). Though still a subject of research in humans, studies in animals and some evidence in people suggest that these pheromonal cues influence mating behaviour, social bonding, and emotional states.

The pineal gland, long revered in Eastern traditions as the seat of higher perception, is also connected to the olfactory system. Though it is not directly stimulated by scent, its functioning is regulated by light and rhythm, both of which are deeply interwoven with breath and smell in yogic practices. When the breath is regulated through *prāṇāyāma* and sacred scents are introduced, such as camphor, frankincense, and agarwood, the body's neuroendocrine system begins to shift. The heart rate slows, the stress response subsides, and a deeper awareness begins to dawn. The scent becomes a vehicle of stillness, guiding the nervous system into parasympathetic balance, where healing and insight are most available.

Scientific studies have confirmed this link. In 2003, a research team led by Herz and Schooler published a study in Nature Neuroscience, which found that odour cues are more emotionally evocative and persistent in memory than those from any other sensory modality. Another study, published in Frontiers in Behavioural Neuroscience in 2015, found that exposure to familiar, comforting smells can measurably reduce cortisol levels—the body's primary stress hormone—and increase parasympathetic nervous activity. This confirms what every spiritual seeker instinctively knows: that scent can soothe the soul even when words fail.

In spiritual traditions, this understanding was never purely intellectual. For instance, in *Śaiva Tantra*, specific *gandhas* (fragrances) were taught to activate particular *tattvas*, or energetic elements. The scent of white lotus was used to open the *sahasrāra*, while musk was said to arouse the *mūlādhāra*. The burning of guggul resin was believed to purify psychic impurities, and jasmine oil was applied to enhance *bhakti rasa*—the flavour of devotional love. These were not perfuming rituals—they were acts of energy modulation. The smell was both symbol and substance, shaping the consciousness of the practitioner.

Interestingly, even the act of remembering a smell has been shown to activate the same brain regions as physically experiencing it. This phenomenon, known as odour imagery, has been extensively studied by researchers like Gottfried et al., who demonstrated in a 2005 Journal of Neuroscience paper that imagined smells activate the piriform cortex—a primary olfactory region. Spiritually, this suggests that inner smells are as real and transformative as outer ones. This is echoed in yogic texts, where advanced meditation practitioners report that subtle fragrances arise spontaneously—a phenomenon viewed not as a hallucination but as a refined perception of the *prāṇic* body.

All of this affirms one truth: smell is not a passive sense. It is an active thread between form and spirit, body and mind, matter and memory. It is the most intimate sense, entering the body without permission, yet never leaving without leaving a trace. It is the carrier of karma, the fragrance of time, and the first language of belonging.

When we inhale a sacred scent, we are not simply detecting molecules—we are tuning into frequencies of presence. The body responds, the mind softens, and the soul remembers. In this subtle act, physiology and philosophy converge. Smell becomes not just a sensation, but a sacred participation.

Section 3: The Fragrance of Remembrance – Smell, Samskāra, and the Subtle Body

In the realm of spiritual experience, smell occupies a space far more sacred than commonly understood. While often dismissed as a background sense—ephemeral, subjective, and less critical than sight or sound—its symbolic and metaphysical dimensions are deeply embedded in the sacred traditions of India. The *rishis* of ancient times recognised that smell is not just an outer function of the nose, but an inner function of the subtle body, intimately tied to memory, identity, and spiritual presence. In its essence, fragrance is not merely scent—it is *samskāra* made manifest. It is the unspoken language of soul-encoded impressions, rising invisibly to the threshold of awareness, reminding us of who we are and where we came from.

The *Upaniṣadic* sages mapped the body not merely in physical terms but in energetic layers, known as the *pañcakośas*—the five sheaths of human existence: the physical (*annamaya*), the energetic (*prāṇamaya*), the mental (*manomaya*), the wisdom (*vijñānamaya*), and the bliss (*ānandamaya*). According to this framework, smell resides in the gross body but reaches inward, penetrating the *prāṇamaya* and *manomaya kośas.* Here, it begins to stir deeper resonances—not just of physical presence but of ancestral memory, ritual intention, and karmic echoes carried over time.

In Yogic philosophy, smell is associated with *gandha tanmātra,* the subtle element of fragrance, which arises from *pṛithvī tattva,* the earth element. *Pṛithvī* is not merely dirt or soil—it is the foundation of embodiment, the aspect of consciousness that condenses into form. Hence, smell is the first sense to awaken in the developing fetus and often the last to fade at the moment of death. This cyclical nature of smell links it directly to the *samsāric* journey of the soul—birth, death, and rebirth. The scent of the mother's body is the first spiritual signature the infant recognises, forming the substratum of belonging and safety.

Ancient rituals acknowledged this truth by invoking deities not merely through *mantras* or offerings, but through fragrance. The *aguru dhūpa,* the resinous incense extracted from the agarwood tree, was burned to invite divine presence. The smell was believed to cleanse not only the space but the aura (*prabhāmaṇḍala*) of the practitioner. In *tantric pūjās,* different scents are assigned to invoke different deities. Jasmine may call forth Kāmadeva or the aspect of beauty in Śrī Devī. Sandalwood is used for calmness, ascension, and clarity, and is often offered to Śiva. Musk symbolises power, mystery, and depth, offered in rites that seek to dissolve egoic boundaries.

More than aesthetic, these fragrances act upon the subtle memory field of the *sādhaka,* penetrating the *manomaya kośa* and stirring latent *samskāras.* Just as sound in the form of *mantra* stirs subtle vibrations that liberate psychic knots, so too does smell, unconsciously awakening buried impressions, both karmic and ancestral. In this way, smell becomes a spiritual excavator, unearthing the deeper terrain of one's being. This is why, during intense *sādhana*, one may encounter sudden scents—floral, pungent, or unknown—with no external source. These are not hallucinations but the olfactory unveiling of spiritual memory.

The *Mahāpurāṇas* describe how divine beings manifest themselves through fragrance. The *Bhāgavata Purāṇa*, for instance, narrates that when Lord Kṛṣṇa entered the homes of His devotees, the air was instantly filled with the scent of sandal and lotus. This scent was not physical—it was the soul's recognition of presence. Similarly, the Liṅga Purāṇa recounts that when Śiva is pleased, the subtle body of the devotee begins to exude a sweet, mystic scent, even if the physical body has not been bathed. This is not a metaphor. This is a description of the *samskāra* field releasing purity, a fragrance emitted from inner cleansing rather than external effort.

Even in practices related to ancestral worship (*pitṛi yajña*), the offering of fragrant substances holds a central place. The smoke of ghee and rice, mixed with fragrant herbs, becomes the vehicle through which memory is transformed into veneration. The scent rises not only into the air but also into the psychic space of gratitude, allowing the practitioner to touch the presence of those who came before. In many families, the scent of certain flowers or specific incense is still associated with departed elders, and their smell invokes their memory more powerfully than photographs or words. This is not nostalgia—this is spiritual continuity through scent.

According to Swami Rama, a modern Himalayan master, the memory of the soul is not stored solely in the brain but also in the subtle nervous system, particularly along the *suṣumnā nāḍī*. He taught that certain fragrances, especially those sanctified through *mantra*, can awaken dormant impressions and guide the practitioner into meditative absorption. This aligns with the findings of neurotheologians such as Dr. Andrew Newberg, who notes that ritual scent is not merely symbolic but physiologically impactful, synchronising the nervous system into states of transcendence.

In this light, smell is not only a sensory input—it is a trigger for liberation. Every sacred scent encountered during worship, pilgrimage, or meditation becomes stored in the memory not as a mere sensation but as a signature of presence. And when reencountered, even after years, it reactivates that same spiritual space. Thus, fragrance becomes a mnemonic key to eternity.

To understand smell spiritually is to understand that every scent carries a story—a story not only of material composition but of subtle correspondence. The smell of vetiver is not only earthy, it also grounds the mind. The scent of roses not only pleases, it also softens the harshness of karmic influences. The smell of frankincense uplifts not just the mind but the *ātmic* vibration, aligning it to higher receptivity.

In the inner practice of *antar-yāga*—the internalised ritual—fragrance is offered not to an external deity but to the inner flame of awareness. Here, the practitioner visualises sacred scents arising from the heart and offering them into the internal altar of the subtle body. The offering becomes not ritual but remembrance—a return to the eternal presence that underlies all form.

In this way, smell is not sensory background; it is spiritual foreground. It does not follow consciousness; it leads it. And in its silence, it whispers what the mind forgets: that the soul remembers through fragrance what the intellect cannot hold.

This is why, in the highest forms of *sādhana*, the aspirant is advised to become aware of the smell of ego burning, the smell of longing rising, the smell of grace arriving—not as poetic metaphors, but as the soul's real perceptions, known through the nose of the subtle body.

To smell rightly is to sense eternity in the present, to recognise the spirit clothed in the scent of form, to breathe not only air but awareness, and to know, in a single inhalation, that this moment, this memory, and this presence are one.

Section 4: The Breath of the Gods – Fragrance as the Bridge between Worlds

Long before words were written and rituals were codified, fragrance rose from flame. In the silence of the ancient *yajña*, when the fire was kindled not for warmth but for worship, the first offering was not a sound; it was a scent. Ghee, soma, herbs, and sacred woods were placed into the fire not only to burn but to transform, and in their transformation, they released an invisible presence—a fragrance that carried prayer without words to the subtle realms. This was *Gandh*, not as an ornament, but as a divine medium. Smell, for the Vedic seer, was not a passive sensation; it was a life-force made fragrant, a thread connecting matter to the unseen.

The Ṛgveda, the most ancient of the Vedas, offers numerous hymns in which fragrance is inseparable from divinity. The offerings to Agni, the divine fire, are spoken of in fragrant terms, for Agni does not merely consume; he carries. He is the mouth of the gods, and through his flames, aroma becomes a means of access.

"त्वं ह्यग्ने प्रथमो अङ्गिरस्तमः ऋत्विजा जातवेदः कवेऽद्य।
स त्वं नो देव यजथाय शर्मणे सृजा पवित्रं सुमनाः स्वस्तये॥"

(Ṛgveda 1.26.1)

You, O Agni, are the foremost of seers, the wise priest, the knower of all. For our well-being, create a purified path—full of fragrance and favour.

The Sanskrit term *sumanāḥ*, often translated as "benevolent," also evokes the sweetness of scent and mind. This association appears frequently in the Vedas, where inner purity is always reflected in outward fragrance. Thus, aroma becomes a mirror of consciousness. A being whose presence carries fragrance is considered one who is *sattvic*, refined, and awakened. The unseen aura becomes olfactory—a phenomenon described in both scripture and spiritual biography.

Smell, in this light, becomes not a sense, but a sign. It is the subtle proof of inner fire, the residual print of presence. Yogic literature, especially within the *Śaiva* and *Tantric* lineages, describes how fragrance arises spontaneously during intense *sādhana*, not due to any material incense, but from the purification of the *nāḍīs*, the energy channels of the subtle body. When the inner fire of *kuṇḍalinī* is awakened, and the blocks in the *cakras* begin to dissolve, practitioners often describe scents of flowers, earth, or divine *attar* rising from within. These experiences, though impossible to verify outwardly, are consistently reported across cultures and centuries.

In the Kaṭha Upaniṣad, Yama, the lord of death, teaches Naciketā that the Self is not found through mere ritual but through refinement of the subtle senses. And in one of the great verses of the Atharvaveda, the power of fragrance is tied directly to healing and transcendence:

"गन्धर्वाणां च पुष्पाणि सुगन्धीनि च यानि वै।
तानि ते प्राहराम्यद्य वायुना सह देवया॥"

(Atharvaveda 9.6.16)

The fragrant flowers of the ***Gandharvas****, those blessed with a sweet aroma, I offer them to the divine wind, may they carry our spirit to the gods.*

Here, the Gandharvas, celestial beings associated with music and fragrance, become symbols of fragrant consciousness, of a realm scented with spirit. The wind, *vāyu*, is not merely breath—it is *vāta*, the subtle energy that moves through body and cosmos, and when joined with *gandha*, it becomes a vehicle of transcendence.

This understanding permeates *Tantric* ritual, where smell is used to summon, dissolve, and deepen. In the *Śrī Vidyā* tradition, practitioners begin each *pūjā* with the offering of *gandha*—often *chandan* (sandalwood), *kastūri* (musk), or *agaru* (aloeswood)—not simply to please the deity, but to activate the space and align inner vibration with outer atmosphere. The scent is the threshold, the subtle invitation that precedes *mantra*, gesture, and form.

The *gandha pūjā*, or worship through scent, is considered among the most refined. In this practice, no words may be spoken. The practitioner applies sandal paste to the forehead of the deity or gently wafts fragrant smoke, not with the mind, but with the breath aligned to awareness. It is said that the deity responds not to the act, but to the presence infused within the act, and smell is its most immediate expression. The *Śaiva Āgamas* note that "where there is scent, there the deity is pleased." Why? Because smell lingers. Long after the light is extinguished and the chant has faded, the fragrance remains, as if marking a trail back to the divine.

Even in meditation, certain schools advocate the use of aroma to anchor awareness. The Nāthas speak of *"ānanda gandha,"* the scent of bliss that arises during states of *samādhi.* Unlike external fragrance, this scent does not fade. It arises within, as the soul's perfume, distilled through *tapas* and inner stillness. It is said that realised saints emit a soft scent that draws devotees even when the saint remains silent. This is not aura; this is olfactory *darśana*, the smell of liberation.

Modern studies give partial support to these claims. Research on meditative states conducted by institutions such as the National Institute of Mental Health and Neurosciences (NIMHANS) has observed that long-term practitioners of breath-based meditations develop heightened olfactory sensitivity. Functional MRI scans reveal that the limbic system, particularly the amygdala and hippocampus, becomes more responsive to olfactory cues when individuals are trained in mindful breathing and smell awareness. While science may not confirm the mystical dimensions, it does indeed affirm that the mind and scent are inextricably linked.

In death rituals, too, fragrance plays a crucial role. The departed are anointed with sandal, ghee, and camphor. The cremation ground is made fragrant, not to mask decay but to signal transition. As the body returns to earth, the scent is the soul's last garland. In Śiva temples, even today, the offering of incense at dusk is performed with eyes closed—not as a gesture of escape, but as a recognition of the invisible, of the subtle world that fragrance always points to.

To live spiritually with the sense of smell is to live attuned to that which lingers. It is to feel presence without seeing it, to know memory without retrieving it, to move with the gods without needing their names. It is to walk not by light alone, but by scented awareness—a mode of knowing that remembers that the soul is not born from thought, but from breath, and that every breath carries a signature, a sacred fragrance, calling us back to where we never truly left.

Section 5: Smell and the Subtle Realms – From Earthly Aroma to the Fragrance of Liberation

There are thresholds we cross in silence—moments when the body still breathes, but the breath no longer carries ordinary air. Instead, it bears something finer, an almost imperceptible fragrance that seems to come not from the world but from within the soul. It is in these moments—deep meditation, profound love, sacred transition, or the nearness of death—that smell transcends its physiological boundaries and enters the realm of the subtle. Here, aroma is no longer a stimulus—it is a spiritual signature. It does not arise from objects but from being itself. It becomes a presence, a memory, a trace of the eternal. This section explores that sacred passage—from earthly aroma to the fragrance of liberation.

The journey of smell begins with the gross body, but it does not end there. In the Vedic understanding, the human being is composed of three bodies: the *sthūla śarīra* (gross body), the *sūkṣma śarīra* (subtle body), and the *kāraṇa śarīra* (causal body). Smell, as a sense, operates across all three. In the gross body, it functions through the olfactory system. In the subtle body, it carries *samskāras*—latent impressions of past experiences. And in the causal body, it is an archetype, a distilled essence of identity. This is why spiritual practitioners often report distinct, unearthly aromas during deep inner states—scents that cannot be traced to any physical source but are experienced with clarity and emotion. These are not hallucinations but sensory echoes of the subtle self.

Modern science, particularly neuroscience and cognitive psychology, provides surprising validation for this ancient view. In a 2009 study published in *Nature Reviews Neuroscience*, author Jay A. Gottfried explored the unique role of the piriform cortex and orbitofrontal cortex in processing olfactory stimuli. Unlike other sensory modalities, smell activates emotion and memory centres before conscious interpretation, evoking what is known in psychology as pre-semantic affect. This knowing is felt before it is understood. This aligns with the *Tantric* idea that *gandha* (scent) operates beneath cognition, touching what the Yogic scriptures call the *chitta*, the deep subconscious pool of impressions.

This process also supports the psychological theory of embodied cognition—the idea that the body does not merely house the mind but participates in its thinking and memory. In the work of cognitive scientist Lawrence Barsalou, we find the proposition that sensory modalities are integral to conceptual understanding. This means smell is not only reactive but constructive—it builds our inner world, not just in memory, but in meaning. A fragrance, even a subtle or imagined one, can shift the entire emotional and spiritual tone of consciousness.

One of the most profound applications of this understanding lies in end-of-life states and spiritual transition. In the traditions of both Śaiva and Buddhist *Tantra*, it is said that when a being attains liberation, or when a realised master leaves the body, a distinct fragrance pervades the space. This is not a cultural myth but a recorded testimony across centuries. In Tibetan Buddhism, the phenomenon is known as zangtal, the arising of a "clear light scent" at the moment of death or realisation. In Hindu hagiographies, such as the accounts of Ramana Maharshi or Lahiri Mahasaya, disciples often describe a mysterious, unearthly fragrance manifesting at the moment of *mahāsamādhi*. These reports are remarkably consistent, pointing to a more profound truth: that liberation has a fragrance, and that this fragrance is not a symbol but a manifestation of consciousness shedding its density.

Psychologically, this may relate to what is termed the limbic release—a neurochemical shift in the brain during altered states of consciousness, wherein the body emits unique combinations of volatile compounds. Dr. Rachel Herz, a neuroscientist who studies olfaction and emotion, notes that smell can also trigger autobiographical meaning that transcends language. When paired with heightened states of awareness, it may form what Jungian psychologists call a numinous experience—a moment of sacred recognition that involves both body and spirit. These are not mere psychological events—they are integrated spiritual awakenings, often marked by the presence of scent.

But why would liberation carry a fragrance? The answer lies in what scent truly is: the release of subtle essence. Just as the scent of a flower is not its outer form but its internal life made perceptible, so too is the fragrance of *mokṣa*, the distillation of the soul's freedom, not seen or heard, but smelled. It is the final perfume of the individual dissolving into the infinite.

In *Tantric* thought, the release of fragrance is associated with the *cakra* system. Each *cakra* is linked to a specific elemental vibration and sense organ. The *mūlādhāra cakra*, associated with earth, governs the sense of smell. But as *kuṇḍalinī* rises, this earthly scent becomes more refined. By the time energy reaches the *ājñā* and *sahasrāra cakras*, the practitioner may no longer be affected by external smells, but will generate inner fragrance. In the texts of Swami Sivananda and Satyananda Saraswati, the occurrence of subtle fragrance is described as a milestone in *sādhana*—a sign that the *prāṇic* body is being purified, and that karmic residues are being sublimated into *sattvic* vibration.

This aligns with the Vedantic view that smell is the most *tamasic* of the senses—the most bound to materiality—but also, when transformed, the most enduring. In meditation, it is often the last sense to withdraw, and the first to return. It is the most loyal of the senses, and thus the most reflective of inner state. To awaken spiritually through scent is to pass through the densest layer of embodiment and emerge into fragrant awareness, the smell of what remains when all else is gone. And what does this mean for the seeker?

It means that every breath is sacred, that every fragrance carries potential for awakening and that the world is not inert matter, but a perfumed spirit. The scent of jasmine, the burning of incense, the aroma of sandalwood—they are not reminders of the sacred. They are the sacred, moving through time, asking only to be received with awareness. To breathe them is to inhale memory, not of past events, but of the eternal self that never forgot.

The path of smell is not loud. It does not declare itself. It whispers. It waits. But when followed to its end, it leads not into the world, but through the world into presence. And in that presence, one realises: liberation is not elsewhere; it is here, it is now, and it is fragrant.

This is the final aroma, not of objects, but of being, not of the senses, but of the soul. It is the fragrance of liberation—silent, lingering, and unmistakable.

Chapter 7

Taste – The Flavor of Awareness

Section 1: The First Offering – Taste as Embodied Presence

Before we speak, before we walk, before we name the world, we taste it. The infant knows the mother not through sight or voice, but through the warmth and flavour of her body. Taste is the earliest intimacy—a silent communion between life and its source. It is the most embodied sense, located not on the skin or in the eye but inside us, deep within the mouth, the tongue, the throat. Taste is not just the identification of flavours—it is the invitation to experience the world from within. It is through taste that we first learn what nourishes and what harms, what draws us close and what we reject. But beyond this biological function lies a more profound truth: taste is the first experience of union, of merging self with world.

The science of taste begins with the gustatory system, a marvel of neurochemical precision. The tongue is home to thousands of tiny sensory structures called papillae, within which lie taste buds—clusters of gustatory receptor cells. These cells respond to five basic taste qualities: sweet, sour, salty, bitter, and umami. Once stimulated, they send signals through the facial (VII), glossopharyngeal (IX), and vagus (X) cranial nerves to the nucleus of the solitary tract in the brainstem. From there, information ascends to the thalamus and finally to the gustatory cortex, where the sensation is interpreted. However, the journey of taste does not end with perception. It continues to the limbic system, particularly the amygdala and hypothalamus, where it becomes emotion, memory, and meaning.

This deep integration of taste and feeling is why a single bite can evoke memories of childhood, why a ritual sip of consecrated water can bring tears, and why fasting is not merely abstention but a form of spiritual sensitivity. In both yoga and *Āyurveda*, taste is classified according to the *rasa* system—not just a taxonomy of flavours, but a spectrum of experience that shapes the body and mind. The six *rasas*—*madhura* (sweet), *amla* (sour), *lavaṇa* (salty), *kaṭu* (pungent), *tikta* (bitter), and *kaṣāya* (astringent)—are not only nutritional but also energetic signatures. Each one carries a vibrational quality that affects the *doṣas*, the mind, and ultimately, the spiritual orientation of the being.

Sweetness grounds and nourishes; bitterness purifies; pungency ignites. These effects are not metaphoric—they are lived realities. Just as food becomes body, flavour becomes being. And here, taste reveals its sacredness. In the Vedas, the preparation and offering of food are central to ritual life. Food is not offered for sustenance alone—it is a sacrifice, a transmission of energy from earth to God, from nature to consciousness.

"अन्नं ब्रह्म रसं ब्रह्म।"

(Annam Brahma, rasam Brahma.)

— *Taittirīya Upaniṣad*

(Food is Brahman; taste is Brahman.)

This statement is revolutionary. It declares that the act of eating is not worldly but divine, and that the sensation of taste is not a distraction from the Self but a gateway to it. *Rasa* is not just a flavour—it is essence, sap, the soul of experience. In Sanskrit aesthetics, *rasa* also refers to the emotional tone evoked by art and poetry. The same word is used for taste and transcendence. This is no coincidence. It points to the central truth that what we taste, we become, and that to taste with awareness is to merge with essence.

In ritual, the offering of taste becomes a form of love. In *naivedya*, the act of offering food to the deity, the devotee does not simply cook—he or she infuses intention into substance, transforming the food into *prāṇa*, into presence. Once offered, the food becomes *prasāda*, a word which means both "grace" and "flavour." *Prasāda* is not merely edible—it is imbued with sanctity, and its taste is said to carry the vibration of the deity to which it was offered.

To eat *prasāda* is not merely to consume food; it is to absorb divinity. This is why taste is so potent in devotion. Saints have spoken of moments when a single spoonful of consecrated water, a trace of tulsi, or a crumb from a sacred offering has transported them into states of ecstasy. The tongue, in these moments, becomes an instrument of reception, not just for nutrients, but for revelation.

In the psychology of taste, this spiritual insight finds its echo. Neurogastronomy, a field pioneered by neuroscientist Gordon M. Shepherd, reveals that taste is not isolated to the tongue but is a multisensory and memory-based phenomenon. Flavour perception, Shepherd argues, is constructed by the brain through a complex synthesis of smell, taste, vision, and expectation. This means that what we taste is as much a memory and belief as it is a sensation. In spiritual practice, this implies that intentionality—what we believe about the taste—can alter our physiological and emotional response to it. A spoonful of ghee taken as medicine may be neutral; the same ghee, offered with a *mantra* and love, becomes nectar.

This brings us to the symbolism of taste in liberation. In the *Bhagavad Gītā*, Kṛṣṇa says:

"रसोऽहमप्सु कौन्तेय।"

(Raso'hamapsu Kaunteya.)

— *Bhagavad Gītā* 7.8

(I am the taste in water, O Kaunteya.)

This simple statement is profound. It declares that taste itself is divinity, that in every drop of water, there is not only refreshment, but remembrance. The Lord does not hide in temples alone. He hides in the sweetness of water, in the tang of tamarind, in the fire of pepper. The one who tastes with awareness does not consume—they commune.

Thus, to awaken through taste is not to indulge but to receive the world as it is—flavoured, fleeting, and full of the divine. It is to stop grasping and begin savouring. It is to let go of judgement and open to the moment, not only with the tongue, but with the heart.

Taste teaches presence, humility, and surrender. It reminds us that life is not understood by analysing, but by tasting its essence. And in this act of tasting, done with reverence, we begin to know what the mystics always knew: that the Self is not somewhere else—it is the flavour of all things, waiting to be received.

Section 2: Memory on the Tongue – Taste, Emotion, and the Longing for Wholeness

To taste is not merely to sample the world—it is to enter it. Of all the senses, taste is the one that most intimately joins subject and object. The world does not remain outside the taster. It is taken in, dissolved, and becomes indistinguishable from the body that receives it. And yet, in this intensely physical act, there is often something haunting, something incomplete. A flavour may arrive and depart in an instant, yet linger in memory for decades. A favourite dish from childhood, a simple fruit tasted under a tree, or a single sip from a sacred temple offering—all these become embedded not only in the mind but in the soul's longing. They remind us not just of what we once ate, but of what we once were. In this way, taste becomes the memory of belonging, and in spiritual life, it becomes the longing for union.

Psychologically, the connection between taste and emotion is profound. The limbic system, particularly the amygdala and hippocampus, plays a crucial role in forming taste memories. These structures not only encode the sensory details of an experience, but also bind them to emotional states. This is why a dish prepared with love tastes different from one made with indifference—even if the ingredients are identical. As neuroscience increasingly shows, taste is not a mechanical detection of flavour—it is a relational act, deeply influenced by context, emotion, and memory.

Studies by researchers such as Paul Rozin and Rachel Herz have demonstrated that taste is not a static function, but a dynamic experience continually shaped by culture, mood, and memory. A single food item may be regarded with disgust in one context and reverence in another. This psychological flexibility reveals something important: that taste is symbolic. It does not merely tell us about the world—it tells us about ourselves, about where we come from, what we desire, what we fear to lose.

In the Indian spiritual tradition, this symbolism is honoured at every level. The six *rasas* (flavours) are not only taste qualities—they are emotional moods. They parallel the *navarasa* of Indian aesthetics—the nine aesthetic moods—used in dance, poetry, and music to evoke more profound truths. Thus, the bitter taste (*tikta*) is linked not only to digestion, but to detachment and discernment. The sweet taste (*madhura*), so often the centre of offerings to deities, is not only pleasant but also a symbol of divine love, comfort, and grace. When devotees offer sweets to Kṛṣṇa or Gaṇeśa, they are not merely appeasing—they are participating in the sweetness itself, attempting to mirror the *ananda*, the bliss, of the divine.

But this sweetness is not always easily found. In the experience of many seekers, the world often tastes sour, bland, or even bitter—not in a literal sense, but in an existential one. The mind seeks satisfaction, but the flavour of life seems off. This inner hunger is what many mystics refer to as the divine thirst, the taste that cannot be named. It is not the desire for food or pleasure, but the yearning for something that lies beneath all other hungers. It is the longing for wholeness, for being tasted by the divine.

To work with this longing, spiritual traditions worldwide have employed the practice of fasting, not as a punishment, but as a means of purification of perception. In the Indian context, *upavāsa* means "to stay close (*upa*) to the divine (*vāsa*)." By abstaining from taste, the practitioner refines it. When the habitual urge to consume is suspended, the seeker begins to experience subtle flavours—not only in food, but in thought, in silence, in presence. The absence of flavour sharpens the awareness of essence.

This is why saints speak of fasting not as deprivation, but as savouring the unspeakable. In the absence of sweetness, they taste sacred stillness. In the absence of salt, they taste the depth of longing. And in the return to food, every morsel becomes *prasāda*, every drop of water becomes sacred elixir, every grain becomes a poem of nourishment.

In therapeutic psychology, this mirrors the concept of reintroduction and mindful savouring—a method used in treating trauma and eating disorders, where the individual is encouraged to re-engage with taste slowly, allowing the body to feel safe in pleasure. The act of tasting becomes re-integrative, returning fragmented parts of the psyche into presence. In spiritual life, this concept is reflected in yoga, which is the union of perception and consciousness.

Thus, taste becomes a sacred feedback loop. What we consume shapes how we feel, and how we feel shapes how we receive the world. The *Bhagavad Gītā*, ever practical, speaks of this in the context of *sāttvic* eating—food that is prepared with reverence, consumed with gratitude, and digested with awareness. Such food is said to increase life, clarity, strength, and joy. But more than that, it refines the sense of taste itself, allowing the seeker to discriminate-not with judgment, but with wisdom.

And what is the final purpose of taste in spiritual life? It is to teach the soul what is truly nourishing, not just for the body, but for the being, and to discover that behind every flavour is a touch of eternity, a reminder that life is not only to be survived, but to be savoured—not blindly, but with the awareness that each taste is a fleeting echo of the formless.

In this awareness, taste becomes an act of devotion, eating becomes a form of meditation, and the tongue becomes a priest, anointing each moment with presence.

Section 3: Rasānanda – The Divine Taste of Consciousness

To walk the path of spiritual transformation is to refine one's taste slowly, not merely in food or art, but in life itself. It is to shift from craving the heavy flavours of ego and sensation to savouring the subtleties of silence, presence, and divine remembrance. This journey is not one of repression but of elevation, where the earthliest of experiences—eating, tasting, savouring—are transfigured into acts of intimacy with the infinite. In the Indian spiritual traditions, this final flowering of taste is called *rasānanda*—the bliss of the essence, the taste of the Self.

The Sanskrit word *rasa* holds multivalent power. In its most common usage, it means taste or flavour. But in spiritual, aesthetic, and philosophical texts, *rasa* transcends the tongue and becomes the sap of life, the essence of experience, the distilled feeling of truth. It is what the *Upaniṣads* call the joy at the heart of being, the subtle pleasure that arises from the realisation that we are one with what we perceive.

"रसवैतसः। रसं ह्येवायं लब्ध्वाऽनन्दी भवति।"

(Rasavaitasaḥ. Rasaṁ hyevāyaṁ labdhvā'nandī bhavati.)

— *Taittirīya Upaniṣad 2.7.2*

(This being is indeed made of rasa. Having tasted this rasa, one becomes blissful.)

The *Upaniṣadic* sages understood that ultimate fulfilment is not in quantity, but in essence. When we taste the real, we become it. And this tasting is not sensory alone—it is spiritual. It is a direct absorption into consciousness, experienced not as knowledge but as flavour.

In the Bhakti traditions, this idea reaches its most poetic and ecstatic form. The relationship between devotee and deity is not intellectual—it is sensual, emotional, and flavourful. The devotee does not seek to know God abstractly but to taste the sweetness of divine love. In the *Bhāgavata Purāṇa*, Kṛṣṇa is described as the very embodiment of *rasa*. He is not just worshipped—He is tasted, in the soul and on the tongue.

The sixteenth-century saint Rūpa Gosvāmin, in his treatise *Bhakti-rasāmṛta-sindhu*, writes that the essence of *bhakti* is *rasa*—not dry devotion, but a relish of divine intimacy. He defines bhakti-rasa as a flow of ecstatic taste that arises when the heart becomes pure and the senses are surrendered in love. In this *rasa*, the devotee forgets separation, forgets self, and becomes flavoured by God.

"अन्यथा स्वादवर्जित्वात्।"

(*Because there is no other flavour like it.*)

This tasting is not a metaphor. Many saints describe experiences where their bodies respond to divine presence with an actual sweetness in the mouth. In the *līlās* of Rādhā and Kṛṣṇa, the nectar of union is described not in concepts but in flavours. The divine is honey, milk, butter, sugarcane, and more. The descriptions are sensual not to entice, but to elevate desire, to show that when directed toward the divine, even the senses become instruments of liberation.

This is the genius of Indian spirituality—it does not reject the senses but refines them into tools of transcendence. In *Tantric sādhana*, the practitioner uses not just breath and *mantra*, but also subtle tastes as a method of awakening. Sacred alchemical compounds, prepared with herbs and metals, were sometimes used to enhance inner sensitivity, to unlock *bindu-rasa*, the drop of nectar said to reside in the crown of the head. This nectar, once activated through deep meditation or *kuṇḍalinī* awakening, is experienced as a subtle sweetness trickling down the throat—not imagined, but real. It is the taste of the self-dissolving into its essence.

Yogic scriptures such as the *Haṭha Yoga Pradīpikā* speak of this in precise terms: "When the mind is purified by the nectar flowing from the *bindu*, the yogi becomes immortal."

In this tradition, taste is not gross but esoteric. The body becomes an altar, and the tongue becomes the receiver of an inner sacrament.

Even in non-Tantric paths, the practice of tasting with awareness is emphasised. The Buddha taught his disciples to eat slowly, mindfully, without craving. In the *Satipaṭṭhāna Sutta*, one is instructed to be present not only to thoughts and sensations but also to taste. This is because taste is where the ego reveals itself—in clinging, aversion, and judgement. But taste is also where the ego can dissolve—in simplicity, surrender, and silent awareness. When food is eaten with mindfulness, desire becomes discernment, and hunger becomes reverence.

In this way, taste becomes a form of yoga. It unites the tongue with the heart, the body with the soul, the fleeting with the eternal. It becomes a teacher of impermanence—every taste vanishes, and yet it teaches presence. It becomes a mirror of longing—every flavour evokes the deeper hunger for truth, a portal to union—when the soul no longer seeks to consume, but only to savour what is.

To live with this awareness is to rediscover the divine in every bite, every flavour, every breath. It is to walk through the world as a taster of the eternal, not grasping, but receiving, not devouring, but delighting. And in that delight, in that sacred *rasa*, the soul is no longer separate; it has become the flavour of awareness itself.

Section 4: Temple of the Tongue – Sacred Taste in Ritual and Scripture

There are few moments as intimate, as personal, and yet as universally shared in Indian spiritual life as the act of receiving *prasāda*. It is more than food—it is memory, blessing, presence, and taste distilled into one silent, fragrant, fleeting act. To accept *prasāda* into the mouth is to accept the divine into the body, to turn nourishment into communion, and flavour into grace. It is here, in this intersection of sacredness and sensation, that the full spiritual power of taste is revealed—not only as survival or pleasure, but as participation in the divine. The tongue, in this view, becomes a temple, and taste, the ceremony.

In the scriptures of the Vedic and post-Vedic era, taste is repeatedly affirmed not merely as a physical sensation but as a carrier of sacred energy. In the Ṛgveda, taste is associated with *soma*, the divine nectar, which is praised not just for its physical effects, but for its ability to elevate the soul:

"सोमः पवते जनिता मतीनां जनिता दिवो जनिता पृथिव्याः।"

(Somaḥ pavate janitā matīnāṁ janitā divo janitā pṛthivyāḥ.)

— *Ṛgveda 9.96.5*

(Soma, flowing, is the generator of wisdom, the father of heaven and earth.)

Soma is not simply drunk—it is tasted in the tongue and the soul. The taste is symbolic of the entry of divine intelligence into the body. The hymns to *soma* are hymns to *rasa*, to the sacred experience of imbibing the real. In this context, the tongue is not profane—it is the site of divine infusion.

This sacred orientation continues in the *Taittirīya Upaniṣad*, where the *ānandamaya kośa*, the sheath of bliss, is reached only after transcending the sheaths of food, energy, mind, and intellect. But intriguingly, the journey begins with the *annamaya kośa*, the sheath of food. The implication is profound: the road to bliss begins with taste, with honouring what is taken in, with cultivating awareness of the flavour of being.

"अन्नं ब्रह्मेति व्यजानात्।"

(Annam Brahmeti vyajānāt.)

(He realized food is Brahman.)

In this statement, food, and by extension taste, is equated with the supreme reality. The perception of taste, when purified of desire and ego, becomes an experience of Brahman itself.

It is in temple rituals that this understanding finds its most elegant and lived form. The daily routine of a Hindu temple includes *naivedya*, the offering of food to the deity, followed by *prasāda*, the distribution of the same food to the devotees. This exchange is not merely symbolic. The transformation of the food during offering, through *mantra*, *mudrā*, and intention, infuses it with spiritual charge. Taste becomes the medium of transfer, not of calories, but of *śakti.*

Each deity is offered specific tastes. To Kṛṣṇa, *madhura rasa*—sweet taste—is supreme, as it mirrors the *rasa of līlā*, divine play. To Śiva, *kaṣāya* (astringent) and *tikta* (bitter) are offered, symbolising detachment and inner purity. In *Śākta* traditions, Devi is often offered spicy and rich foods—*lavaṇa* and *kaṭu rasas*—as expressions of her dynamic, transformative power. These associations are not arbitrary—they are embodied theology. The deity does not consume food but receives its essence, and the devotee, in turn, consumes what remains infused with divinity.

In *Tantric* rites, the symbolism deepens. The act of consuming consecrated food or drink becomes a part of the *pañcamakāra* rituals, where even sensory pleasure is transformed into a vehicle for awakening. The tongue, usually bound by taste and craving, becomes the site of release, of *tanmatra* transformation, where the subtle essence of taste (*rasa tanmatra*) is returned to its source, or consciousness.

This is why in yogic alchemy, the awakened yogi is said to secrete *amṛita*—a divine fluid tasted not through the mouth, but in the palate of consciousness. In advanced *kuṇḍalinī* practices, as the energy rises and purifies the *cakras*, it reaches the *bindu visarga*, located at the back of the head, and releases a subtle sweetness, described as divine nectar, which, when tasted, brings bliss, detachment, and intuitive knowledge.

"यस्मिन् सर्वाणि भूतानि आत्मैवाभूद्विजानतः।"

(Yasmin sarvāṇi bhūtāni ātmaivābhūd vijānataḥ.)

— *Bṛhadāraṇyaka Upaniṣad 4.5.14*

(For the one who knows, all beings become the Self.)

This realisation, when embodied, is not just intellectual—it is tasted. The sage becomes sweet, not just in conduct, but in presence. It is said that the speech of a *jñānī* (realised one) tastes sweet, that the air around them is soft, and the atmosphere nourishing. This sweetness is not metaphor—it is a subtle fragrance of presence, transmitted through speech, breath, and yes, taste.

To live in this way is to live as if every moment is *prasāda*—every interaction, every meal, every emotion is an offering. The tongue becomes a witness, not a judge; it no longer demands, but receives. And in receiving, it dissolves the ego that separates, the mind that seeks to classify, and the craving that causes suffering.

Thus, taste returns us to the centre of experience, to the first act of existence: to taste the world and to say, "This, too, is the Divine."

Section 5: Beyond the Tongue – Taste and the Dissolution into Silence

There is a moment in every journey when the traveller forgets the road. The goal dissolves, the effort stops, and what remains is simply presence—still, luminous, aware. In the journey of taste, this moment comes when flavour itself disappears, not into blandness, but into fullness —a state where the seeker no longer tastes sweetness or bitterness, devotion or detachment, but instead experiences a pure awareness untouched by sensation. This is the final *rasa*, the flavour of the unconditioned, the taste of liberation, and it arrives not with consumption, but with surrender.

Taste, like all the senses, is dual by design. It functions on contrast—sweet versus salty, sour against bitter. Yet spiritual realisation begins where contrast ends. As the *sādhaka* matures, the dualities of taste begin to lose their grip. The mind no longer seeks particular flavours in food, people, or experience. Instead, it begins to rest in the flavour of being itself—a taste not located on the tongue, but in the soul. This transition is not theoretical; it is deeply experiential, it is when the food becomes incidental, and the act of tasting becomes an act of recognition: not "I taste this," but "This, too, is the Self."

The ancient sages described this not as deprivation but as a new kind of fullness. In the *Bṛhadāraṇyaka Upaniṣad*, the realised one is said to no longer chase tastes, yet is nourished by everything. The realised being becomes *rasa-siddha*—one who is established in essence. This is echoed in the *Bhagavad Gītā*, where Kṛṣṇa tells Arjuna:

"यदृच्छालाभसंतुष्टो द्वंद्वातीतो विमत्सरः।"

(Yadṛcchā-lābha-santuṣṭo dvandvātīto vimatsaraḥ.)

— *Gītā 4.22*

(One who is content with what comes by chance, who is beyond dualities and free from envy.)

Such a one is beyond sweetness and bitterness, not because they deny taste, but because they have tasted the root of all flavour, and it has brought them peace.

In yogic literature, the role of the *Guru* becomes essential, as it is the *Guru* who awakens the seeker not just to truth, but to subtlety. In the presence of the *Guru,* the crude senses are refined. The *Guru* does not teach what to taste, but how to taste without clinging. Under the *Guru's* gaze, every flavour—joy or sorrow, gain or loss—becomes *prasāda.* In this state, life itself is understood as a consecrated meal, and the seeker is no longer a consumer but a recipient of the sacred.

This refinement through the *Guru's* presence is mirrored in the discipline of *yogic sādhana.* As one purifies the body and mind, the tongue too becomes purified—not through denial, but through awareness. What once tasted heavy or aggressive begins to feel disruptive. What once felt bland now reveals its subtleties. In time, the *sādhaka* becomes sensitive not only to food but to speech, thought, and even silence. Silence becomes the finest taste of all—one that carries no calories, no form, but leaves the deepest nourishment.

Here, the symbolic merges with the metaphysical. In the highest states of meditation, advanced practitioners report a flavour that is not sensory but existential — a kind of subtle sweetness, often described as honey or nectar — arising spontaneously. It is not of the tongue, yet it is tasted. It is not given, yet it is received. This is amṛita, the nectar of immortality—not in mythology, but in direct realisation.

This experience is not limited to ascetics or mystics. It lives in the quiet moments of anyone who has ever experienced the flavour of stillness, the richness of a shared silence, and the aftertaste of a sacred moment. It is when the senses pull inward and the heart expands. It is when life no longer needs spice to feel vibrant. It is the flavour of the eternal, hiding in simplicity.

And so, the journey of taste ends not in fullness or emptiness, but in knowing that everything the tongue ever longed for was pointing back to the soul's desire to remember its essence. Every flavour, every meal, every craving, was a hint, a whisper, a trail of breadcrumbs leading back to the Self.

To awaken to this is to realise that the great feast of existence is not outside us. It is our very nature. And the flavour of that nature, when known, is enough. It is still, it is whole, it is sacred.

It is awareness made edible.

Chapter 8

Intuition – The Sixth Sense

Section 1: The Silent Knowing – Awakening the Inner Perception

There is a knowing that comes without thinking. It arrives without proof, without argument, without cause. It is not summoned by logic or analysis, but it stands firmer than fact. It does not speak loudly, yet it cannot be ignored. This is intuition—the subtle and sacred art of perceiving what lies beneath, before, or beyond the senses. It is the sixth sense, not as an extension of physical perception, but as its transcendence. It is that mysterious faculty that whispers from the quiet centre of the soul, where reason bows to resonance, and certainty arises from stillness.

In Sanskrit, intuition is often associated with *prājña, viveka,* or *antar-jñāna*—inner knowing. It is not blind impulse or fleeting emotion, but a deeper cognitive awareness that emerges from inner stillness and refined perception. The *Upaniṣads* often speak of this knowing, not as something one learns, but as something one remembers, as if the soul is already in possession of all truth, and the work of life is to uncover it.

"तं तु सत्येन तपसा योगेन नित्यं
अन्तःशरीरे ज्योतिर्मयो हि शुभ्रः।"

(Taṁ tu satyena tapasā yogena nityaṁ
antaḥśarīre jyotirmayo hi śubhraḥ.)

—*Śvetāśvatara Upaniṣad 2.15*

(Through truth, austerity, and constant yoga, that inner luminous being is seen, resplendent within the body.)

The verse speaks not of vision with the eyes, but of perception from the heart —a seeing that arises when the self is purified and centred. This *jyotirmaya*, this inner light, is the seat of intuition.

Physiologically, intuition is often dismissed as ineffable; yet, recent neuroscience has begun to study the mechanisms behind such non-linear knowing. Researchers such as Antonio Damasio have proposed the somatic marker hypothesis, suggesting that the body itself carries a form of intelligence—a memory and anticipatory knowledge that informs decision-making without the mediation of the rational mind. These signals arise from visceral processing and emotional integration, activating regions such as the insula and anterior cingulate cortex, both of which are highly active in meditation and states of heightened awareness. In essence, intuition is not unscientific—it is a subtle science, a blend of sensory data, unconscious pattern recognition, and emotional insight.

However, Indian philosophy has consistently elevated intuition to the pinnacle of spiritual development. The journey of the seeker does not end with sensory mastery but culminates in the awakening of *prajñā*, the capacity to know directly. In the Bhagavad Gītā, Kṛṣṇa tells Arjuna:

"बुद्धियोगं उपाश्रित्य मच्चित्तः सततं भव।"

(Buddhiyogaṁ upāśritya mac-cittaḥ satataṁ bhava.)

— *Gītā 10.10*

(Take refuge in the yoga of wisdom, and constantly be absorbed in Me.)

Here, "buddhiyoga" refers not merely to intellect, but to intuitive wisdom —the silent force that, when purified, leads to unity with the divine.

In yogic practice, intuition is cultivated through *pratyāhāra* (withdrawal of senses), *dhyāna* (meditation), and ultimately *samādhi* (absorption). When the sensory inputs are stilled, the inner vision begins to shine. This is why *yogis* often speak of a sense of direction, knowing when to act, speak, move, or when to remain still, without any logical cause. These are not guesses. They are inner promptings from the Self, which, unclouded by ego or noise, see clearly.

The *āgamas* and *tantras* elaborate this further. In Śaiva traditions, the *Guru* is described as *jñānadāyakaḥ*, the one who bestows direct knowledge, not through words alone, but through presence, gaze, and silence. The transmission of knowledge without instruction, known as *śaktipāta*, is the awakening of inner intuition. The disciple begins to know, not because the *Guru* explained, but because the barriers to knowing are dissolved.

"गुरुः साक्षात् परं ब्रह्म।"

(The Guru is verily the Supreme Reality.)

Why? Because the *Guru*, established in Self, becomes the mirror of the intuition within us.

In practical terms, intuition begins to express itself in alignment. The individual finds that choices become effortless, marked by a flow and resonance. Obstacles are met not with resistance but with clarity. This is the mark of one whose *antar-jñāna* is alive. They may not know the details, but they walk with trust in the whisper within. This trust is not blind—it is born of contact with the inner *guru*, the divine presence that watches from the cave of the heart.

To cultivate intuition, then, is not to develop a skill, but to refine the soul. It is to quiet the mind, to purify desire, to ground the senses, and to allow the Self to speak in its language, not words, but knowing. It is to return to that place where the first sound was heard, the first light seen, and the first flavour of truth tasted—before the world became loud.

In this return, intuition becomes not just a sense, but the bridge to the divine. It is not added—it is remembered. It is not taught—it is revealed. And once it awakens, the seeker is never lost again. For the voice of truth, once heard within, becomes the only compass worth following.

Section 2: Gut, Dream, and the Hidden Voice – Messages from Beyond the Mind

There are moments when we know something without knowing how we know it. We turn down a street we have never walked and feel uneasy. We meet a stranger and sense either closeness or caution before a word is spoken. We wake from a dream with a clarity that defies explanation. These are not accidents. They are the subtle signals of the soul, arriving through what psychology calls the unconscious, and what spiritual traditions have long honoured as the inner voice, the *ātmā's* whisper, the mind beneath the mind. In this realm, intuition is not mysterious—it is native. It is the body's way of listening, the psyche's way of guiding, and the spirit's way of remembering what the intellect has forgotten.

Science has only recently begun to catch up with what mystics have long affirmed: that beneath the rational surface of the brain lies a vast ocean of implicit knowing. Psychologists such as Carl Jung understood dreams, synchronicities, and gut instincts not as irrational phenomena, but as expressions of what he termed the collective unconscious—a deep psychic reservoir shared across all human beings. This unconscious is not just memory—it is mythic, symbolic, and archetypal. It speaks in signs, feelings, and dreams. And when we listen to it, we align not only with ourselves but with the deeper fabric of life itself.

Gut feelings—those visceral reactions in the stomach or chest—are among the most common expressions of this hidden intelligence. They arise before thought, often in high-stakes or emotionally charged situations. Neuroscientist Antonio Damasio, in his work on decision-making, has demonstrated that these "somatic markers" are vital to human choice. The gut, rich in nerve endings and often referred to as the second brain, processes input faster than conscious reasoning. It gathers cues from body language, tone, facial micro-expressions, even environmental changes, and renders a judgment without words. This is intuition grounded in the body.

However, while science points to biological mechanisms, Indian spiritual traditions take it a step further. The gut is not just a processing centre—it is a spiritual organ, located in the region of the *maṇipūra cakra*, the third energy centre associated with power, discernment, and will. When balanced, this *chakra* grants the seeker clarity of direction. When disturbed, it leads to confusion, fear, and craving. Thus, gut instinct is not simply a neurochemical phenomenon—it is an energetic sensitivity. It is the *prāṇic* body registering the vibrations of people, places, and possibilities, and offering guidance from within.

Similarly, dreams have always been portals of intuition. In the Vedas, dreams are not dismissed as nonsense but categorised—some as psychic residue, others as prophetic, and still others as divine visitations. In the *Bṛihadāraṇyaka Upaniṣad*, dreams are discussed as journeys of the soul, moments when the conscious mind sleeps but the deeper self remains alert, exploring dimensions that the waking eye cannot see.

"यदा तु सुप्तो न किञ्चन पश्यति स उ तदा भवति।"

(Yadā tu supto na kiñcana paśyati sa u tadā bhavati.)

— *Bṛhadāraṇyaka Upaniṣad 4.3.19*

(When one sleeps and sees nothing, then he becomes one with that.)

Here, "that" is Brahman, the ground of all being. The implication is that deep sleep and dreams are spiritual thresholds, and the symbols that arise in dreams are not random—they are messages from our eternal nature, clothed in metaphor.

Mystics across cultures agree. Saint Teresa of Ávila, Ramakrishna Paramahamsa, and Rumi all describe dreams as realms of spiritual encounter. In their dreams, they met guides, received teachings, and awakened new capacities. Rumi referred to dreams as the whispers of the soul at night, and Ramakrishna instructed his disciples to observe their dreams, for in them, "Mother speaks."

Modern psychology, too, recognises this power. Therapists working in Jungian analysis or transpersonal psychology often treat dreams not as symptoms, but as spiritual maps—offering clues, warnings, and confirmations. Dreams bypass the censor of the waking mind and speak directly to the symbolic imagination, where intuition resides.

Likewise, hunches—those sudden insights or inexplicable certainties—are often dismissed as coincidence. But spiritual literature views them as the soul's flashlights, brief illuminations from a deeper intelligence. Shankaracharya, in his commentaries, referred to *vijñāna*—a level of knowledge that is direct, spontaneous, and transformative. This is not the knowledge of books, but of contact, resonance, and immediacy.

To cultivate this intuitive faculty is not to reject logic, but to transcend its limitations. Logic can only operate on known variables. Intuition, on the other hand, reaches into the unknown, into the field of possibility that lies just beyond current perception. And here, the *sādhanā* of silence becomes crucial. Whether through meditation, *mantra*, or *māunam* (vow of silence), the seeker begins to hear the subtle voice beneath the noise. Intuition does not shout—it waits. It speaks in the spaces between thoughts. To access it, one must learn to dwell in those spaces.

And what is the fruit of listening? It is alignment. The intuitive person does not avoid mistakes but walks with a kind of grace, a rhythm that feels guided. They may not know where they are going, but they move as if they are led. They trust not because they are naïve, but because they are in tune with the body, the unconscious, the divine.

To honour gut feelings, dreams, and hunches is to trust the architecture of the soul—a design far older and wiser than our fleeting thoughts. It is to know that the divine speaks not only in thunder or flame, but also in the flutter in the belly, the image behind the eyelids, and the sudden certainty without cause. These are the messages from beyond the mind, and when we listen, we no longer walk alone. We walk with the Self.

Section 3: The Eye within – Inner Vision and the Third Eye of Intuition

There is a seeing that is not done with the eyes. It does not depend on light, angle, or form. It arises in silence, behind closed lids, and offers images not of the world but of the truth behind the world. This is the seeing of the inner eye, the third eye, the intuitional center that does not perceive surfaces but penetrates essences. Known in yogic tradition as the ājñā cakra, this center of perception is not physical, yet it governs vision at the most subtle level. It is the seat of clarity, insight, discrimination, and spiritual knowing. It is not fantasy or imagination—it is antar-darśana, the sacred act of seeing the Self.

The Sanskrit word dṛṣṭi means "sight," but in yogic philosophy, it refers not merely to the act of looking, but to the quality of consciousness that enables seeing. The most refined dṛṣṭi is not outward-facing but inward-facing: divya dṛṣṭi, or divine sight. This is the eye that Arjuna was granted when he asked Kṛṣṇa to reveal his cosmic form in the Bhagavad Gītā:

"दिव्यं ददामि ते चक्षुः पश्य मे योगमैश्वरम्।"

(Divyaṁ dadāmi te cakṣuḥ paśya me yogam aiśvaram.)

— *Gītā 11.8*

(I give you divine sight—behold my majestic yoga.)

Kṛṣṇa makes it clear that normal eyes are insufficient. To perceive the divine, one needs a new kind of sight—**the inner eye**, refined by purity, discipline, and surrender.

This third eye is not a metaphor. It has been identified in the yogic anatomy as the **ājñā cakra**, located at the space between the eyebrows. Energetically, it is associated with the **pineal**

gland, a small endocrine structure deep within the brain, long thought to be a vestigial organ but now understood to play a role in circadian rhythms, melatonin secretion, and possibly even altered states of consciousness. Philosophers from **Descartes**, who called it the "seat of the soul," to modern neuroscientists like **Rick Strassman**, who researched its connection to endogenous DMT (a powerful consciousness-altering compound), have suspected that this gland may play a role in **non-ordinary perception**.

In yogic physiology, the ājñā cakra is considered the command center, the bridge between the individual will and the divine will. It governs intuition, vision, mental clarity, **and** inner listening. When it is open and balanced, the seeker experiences lucidity, direction, and perception beyond sensory input. One begins to "see" not the future, but the truth behind appearances. The illusory nature of form becomes apparent, and the play of duality is recognized as precisely that—a play.

Mystical traditions across the globe echo this experience. Christian mystics speak of the "eye of the heart." Sufi poets, such as Rumi, speak of "a window in the chest through which the soul looks at the Beloved." In the Kabbalistic Tree of Life, the third eye corresponds to Da'at, a form of knowledge not taught but revealed. In Buddhist tantra, the development of prajñā (wisdom) allows the practitioner to see the emptiness and luminosity of all phenomena, not through analysis, but through direct inner vision.

But how does one cultivate such sight?

Yogic texts prescribe dhyāna (meditation) and trāṭaka **(gazing)** practices to stabilize awareness and direct it inward. In trāṭaka, the aspirant gazes at a single point—often a flame—until the outer image fades and the inner eye begins to replicate it within the mind's space. Over time, this practice awakens a new faculty: the ability to see without eyes, to perceive truth without distortion.

The Kularnava Tantra, a revered Śaiva text, states:

"सर्वं मनसि दृश्यते तदा साक्षात्परं पदम्।"

(Sarvaṁ manasi dṛśyate tadā sākṣāt paraṁ padam.)

(When all is seen within the mind, then the Supreme Goal is realized directly.)

This inner vision is not a delusion—it is a direct perception of reality, free from sensory interference. It is the state in which dreams become clearer than waking life, where symbols take on luminous significance, and where the boundaries between inner and outer begin to blur.

In psychology, Carl Jung emphasized the value of such inner images, which he called archetypes. He saw the symbols that arose in dreams, visions, and spontaneous inner perception as gateways to what he called the Self—the wholeness beyond the ego. Jung's concept of active imagination, a method of consciously engaging with these inner symbols, parallels ancient meditative practices where the seeker follows the imagery to its source in awareness.

Thus, the inner eye is not a fantasy—it is a cognitive and spiritual organ, activated through purification, silence, and inward-turning. It allows the seeker to move from sensory reality to subtle reality, and ultimately to non-dual awareness, where seer, seen, and sight become one.

When the third eye opens, the world does not vanish—it becomes translucent. Every form reveals its emptiness, every appearance its origin. The veil lifts not in a flash of light, but in a gentle recognition of presence—that what we sought to see was always looking back at us, from within.

Section 3: The Eye within – Inner Vision and the Third Eye of Intuition

There exists within us a faculty that does not depend on external light, a form of seeing that does not require the eyes. It is not a sense in the conventional manner, but a perception that rises when the senses turn inward. This is the inner eye, often referred to as the third eye, the seat of intuitive vision and spiritual discernment. It does not show us the visible world; it reveals the truth behind appearances, the quiet essence of all things. This is not a faculty of imagination or fantasy, but of refined awareness—a sacred sight cultivated in silence, discipline, and deep interiority.

In the tradition of *yoga* and *tantra*, this inner eye is associated with the *ājñā cakra*, located at the point between the eyebrows. It is said to be the seat of command, of perception, of knowing without effort. Energetically, it governs clarity, vision, insight, and direction. Physiologically, it is linked to the pineal gland, a tiny endocrine structure within the brain that regulates circadian rhythms and may play a role in altered states of consciousness. While science is still exploring its full potential, yogic texts have long affirmed that this gland, when awakened, acts as a gateway to inner sight.

When the inner eye is awakened, one no longer looks at the world as merely a collection of objects. Instead, one begins to perceive interconnections, patterns, and subtle energies. This is not to be confused with mere imagination. Inner vision is not fantasy; it is a heightened sensitivity to what is, often described by spiritual practitioners as "seeing in the dark"—a clarity that arises when the noise of the mind subsides.

Mystical traditions across cultures affirm the existence of this faculty. In the Christian tradition, mystics speak of "the eye of the heart." In Sufism, it is referred to as the "window of the soul." In Buddhist meditation, advanced states of insight (*vipassanā*) arise not from thought, but from direct seeing—a clear, silent recognition of impermanence, emptiness, and the essence of being. Across all these traditions, the awakening of inner sight is accompanied by a sense of stillness, awe, and non-dual awareness.

In psychological terms, this form of perception aligns with depth psychology's recognition of the symbolic and archetypal layers of the psyche. Carl Jung, in particular, emphasised the value of engaging with inner images—not as projections or delusions, but as messages from the deeper Self. What arises in dreams, visions, and contemplative states is not random; it is meaningful. And when these images are seen with attention and reverence, they become vehicles of transformation.

The process of cultivating inner sight begins with stilling the outer senses. In yogic practice, this is called *pratyāhāra*—the withdrawal of the senses from the external world. It is followed by *dhyāna*, or meditation, which allows attention to settle inward. Over time, the practitioner begins to experience images, insights, and intuitions not accessible through ordinary thought. These experiences are not to be clung to or dramatised, but to be witnessed with humility, allowing the inner eye to guide rather than entertain.

The inner eye also teaches discernment. As the practitioner grows in sensitivity, they begin to see not only the divine essence of things but also the subtle distortions of ego, illusion, and attachment. This seeing can be both blissful and sobering. It takes courage to face oneself as one truly is. But this courage is rewarded with freedom—a freedom born of clarity, of no longer being deceived by the shifting images of the world or the fluctuations of the mind.

In this state, choices no longer arise from habit, fear, or desire. They emerge from a centred knowing, a deep listening that does not need to ask. Life begins to flow with purpose, not imposed from without, but emerging from within. This is the fruit of inner vision—not mystical imagery or prophetic power, but the quiet confidence that comes from aligning with the deeper currents of reality.

The awakening of the third eye is not an event—it is a gradual unfolding. It happens each time we pause before reacting, each time we turn inward before deciding, each time we trust the still voice rather than the loud world. It grows in silence, ripens in humility, and blossoms in the space where thought has grown quiet.

To live with the inner eye open is not to reject the world, but to see it, transient, luminous, and sacred. It is to look not at the forms alone, but at their essence. And in doing so, to realise that all sight, when cleansed of ego, leads to the same vision: the vision of oneness.

Section 4: Symbol, Vision, and the Sacred Image – The Eye in Myth and Temple

Every culture has symbols that outlive its empires, icons that survive the erosion of language, and visions that persist in the minds of mystics long after their words have faded. These symbols are not artifice—they are echoes of the inner world; fragments of intuition given form. They do not originate from logic or invention but from a deep, unseen reservoir of the psyche. In this way, intuition not only whispers through feelings and dreams—it speaks through symbols. And when we engage with these symbols—whether in temple carvings, sacred texts, or the imagined forms that arise in meditation—we are not merely observing, we are remembering. We are touching the archetypal fabric of consciousness that transcends individual thought.

In the Indian tradition, symbols are not ornamental—they are vehicles of presence. A *yantra* is not just geometry, but a map of consciousness. A deity's image is not a representation—it is a living energy body, a node where the personal and cosmic intersect. These forms did not arise from imagination alone; they arose from vision—from *rishis* and seers who saw not with their eyes but with their inner knowing. The sacred image is a condensation of intuition, a visual *mantra* that carries the power of the formless within the limits of form.

In psychological terms, Carl Jung identified this kind of imagery as emerging from the collective unconscious—the vast layer of the psyche shared across humanity. He found that regardless of time or place, people experienced similar dream figures, sacred geometries, and mythic themes. The reason? These images are not personal—they are archetypal. They belong to the deeper strata of being, and when they rise into awareness, they do so with a force that both stirs and centres. For Jung, these symbols were not decoration but doorways to individuation, the process by which the individual awakens to the Self.

In India, these same principles are reflected in the use of *mūrti*—the sacred form of the deity. When the devotee looks upon the form of Kṛṣṇa, Durgā, or Śiva, they are not engaging in idolatry; they are activating an intuitive recognition. The eye does not merely see the form—the heart remembers the essence. The *mūrti*, consecrated through ritual and *mantra*, becomes a mirror for the intuitive gaze. The devotee sees, and is seen. In that mutual gaze, an inner eye opens.

Temples themselves are constructed as architectures of inner vision. The *garbhagṛiha*, or sanctum sanctorum, is modelled on the womb of consciousness, where the seeker turns inward to face the divine light. The journey through the temple—from the vast outer halls to the dark, intimate sanctum—is symbolic of the path of *pratyāhāra*: the withdrawal of the senses, the turning inward, the approach toward the centre. And at the centre is always a symbol—a light, a form, a flame, not as a distraction, but as an intuitive focus, a point where outer vision dissolves into inner sight.

These sacred symbols often appear spontaneously in meditation or dreams. The image of a lotus, a flame, a serpent, or a divine being may rise without prompting. In such moments, the spiritual practitioner learns not to grasp or dismiss, but to listen. These are not fantasies; they are the soul's language, shaped by archetype and energised by presence. To interpret them is not to decode them intellectually, but to allow them to resonate within the body and breath. Their meaning is not read—it is felt.

In many yogic texts, such as those of the *Nātha* tradition and the *Tantras*, symbols are used not only for contemplation but as seeds of transformation. A *bija mantra* (seed syllable) is itself a symbolic sound, a vibration encoded with intuitive knowledge. When meditated upon deeply, it reveals not concepts, but states of being. Similarly, the Śaiva tradition speaks of *ābhāsa*—the spontaneous radiance of consciousness that first appears as light, then as form, then as recognition. This movement from light to form to meaning is the very mechanism of symbolic intuition.

In the heart of the seeker, this process is alive. A dream image touches a memory. A line from scripture echoes a thought. A symbol in the temple mirrors a vision in meditation. These are not coincidences. They are alignments—evidence that the inner and outer worlds are not separate, but reflections of one underlying intelligence.

And this is the essence of intuitive vision: to see not merely with the eye, but with symbolic depth, to perceive not only the image, but also the essence, to not only engage with form, but also feel the formless moving within it. This vision is not about fantasy—it is about fidelity to presence. It is the ability to recognise the divine signature in every curve of the *mūrti*, in every syllable of a *mantra*, in every silent intuition that rises unbidden.

When this faculty is awakened, the world no longer appears as opaque matter. It becomes mythic, transparent, and alive with meaning. Every form points beyond itself, every sight invites remembrance, and the inner eye, now alert and attuned, begins to see symbol and soul as one.

Section 5: The Eye of Non-duality – Seeing the World as One Light

At the edge of the known, when the senses begin to rest, when the mind releases its grasp on form and name, a new kind of seeing emerges. This is not the seeing of difference, of distance, or of doubt—it is a seeing so quiet, so vast, that what is seen and who sees dissolve into one luminous presence. This is the culmination of intuition. It is no longer the sixth sense—it is no sense at all, for it is beyond sensing. It is the eye of non-duality, where subject and object vanish, and what remains is simply awareness—spontaneous, self-luminous, and indivisible.

In the early stages of spiritual perception, intuition serves as an inner compass, helping to distinguish between what is false and what is true, what is shadow and what is light, and what is self and what is ego. But this discernment still belongs to the realm of duality—it is the voice of clarity within a world of contrast. As it refines, intuition evolves. It no longer discriminates between paths—it becomes the path itself. It no longer identifies what is right—it dissolves the question. What remains is not an answer, but a state of being where division has never existed.

This transition is not a leap—it is an unfolding. Like petals opening to the light, the seeker's awareness grows more subtle and inclusive. First, there is intuition as guidance—gut feelings, inner nudges, glimpses. Then, there is intuition as recognition—a sense of knowing without learning. Finally, there is intuition as unity—a direct, unshakable knowing that there is nothing other than this. It is not a thought; it is not even an experience. It is the abidance in the real, the still, vast field in which all names arise and dissolve.

The *Guru* plays a central role in this transformation, not because the *Guru* imparts new knowledge, but because the *Guru* removes ignorance. The *Guru* is the mirror in which the seeker first sees the formless reflected. In the early stages, the *Guru* is a guide. Later, the *Guru* becomes the goal. Eventually, the *Guru* is known as the Self. But only the intuitive eye can perceive this. It is not the outer form of the *Guru* that liberates, but the transmission of being, the silent resonance that awakens what was always already within.

To reach non-duality through intuition is to cross from seeing to being. When we speak of awakening the third eye, we often think of visions, colours, and lights. But these are signs along the way. The final opening is not spectacular—it is simple. The world is no longer outside. The Self is no longer inside. The gaze turns not outward or inward, but nowhere, for there is no centre and no circumference. Everything is light, and light knows itself by shining.

The sages called this *aparokṣa jñāna*—direct, unmediated knowledge of the Self. It cannot be taught. It cannot be earned. It can only be remembered. And it is intuition, freed from identity and purpose, that becomes the gateway to this remembrance. The final intuition is not a message or sign—it is the realisation that there never was anything but this. This presence, this stillness, this moment, this seeing are done not through a lens, but as the lensless eye of awareness.

When this realisation dawns, life does not change—it is seen as it is. Every form becomes transparent, every sound becomes silence, and every act becomes stillness. The world is not rejected—it is seen as a wave of the same ocean. Duality is not destroyed—it is understood. The dance of difference continues, but the dancer no longer forgets the stage beneath.

This is the eye of non-duality. It sees without separation, without seeking, and without self. And in that seeing, all questions fall away. What remains is not enlightenment—it is light, simply being itself.

Chapter 9

Hormones – The Alchemy Within

To fully understand the role of hormones in the journey toward self-realisation, it is essential to move beyond the compartmentalised view of glandular function and begin to see the endocrine system as a neurochemical orchestra, conducting the interplay between perception, emotion, memory, and transcendence. As research in psychoneuroendocrinology advances, we are beginning to grasp the intimate ways in which endocrine signals influence not only mood and cognition but also spiritual receptivity and states of altered consciousness. The human organism is not a machine governed by isolated parts, but an integrated system where hormones act as the subtle language of alignment, communicating between body, mind, and soul.

Emerging research on the gut-brain-endocrine axis sheds light on this integrative view. Hormones such as ghrelin, leptin, and peptide YY, traditionally associated with appetite regulation, have been shown to influence cognitive function, decision-making, and even spiritual practices like fasting and silence. Ghrelin, for example, increases during fasting and has neuroprotective effects, enhancing hippocampal plasticity and promoting learning. In many monastic traditions across the world—Christian, Buddhist, Jain, and Hindu alike—fasting has long been practised not merely for its health benefits, but for its capacity to induce a state of clarity and inwardness, sharpening both perception and devotion. This ancient insight finds a modern counterpart in the discovery that hormonal fluctuations during fasting can enhance neurogenesis and increase brain-derived neurotrophic factor (BDNF), a protein essential for cognitive health and emotional balance.

The practice of *brahmacarya*—often translated as celibacy but more broadly implying mastery over desire—further exemplifies the conscious regulation of hormonal forces. Sexual energy is not repressed in spiritual practice; instead, it is transmuted. This principle is echoed in *Kundalinī Yoga*, where the ascent of energy through the *suṣumnā nāḍī*—from the *mūlādhāra* (root) to the *sahasrāra* (crown)—is accompanied by hormonal and neurochemical changes. While these transformations have often been described metaphorically, they are increasingly being explored in the context of dopaminergic pathways, endogenous opioid systems, and neuroendocrine feedback loops. The experience of bliss during deep meditation is not imaginary; it correlates with increased levels of serotonin, GABA, anandamide, and other neuromodulators, which collectively reduce anxiety and generate feelings of unity, timelessness, and joy.

These states are not reserved for ascetics alone. Even in ordinary life, when attention is stilled and breath is regulated, the hormonal system shifts. A person sitting in gratitude or reverence, absorbed in music or nature, unknowingly triggers a cascade of endocrine responses: lowered cortisol, increased oxytocin, stabilised insulin, and elevated endorphins. Such shifts point to the profound plasticity of the human organism—our capacity to adapt not only to environmental stimuli but to states of consciousness. Hormones, in this light, become instruments of attunement, aligning physiology with the inner state of the seeker.

Equally vital is the role of thyroid hormones, which modulate metabolism and energy regulation. Thyroxine (T_4) and triiodothyronine (T_3) influence cellular oxygen consumption, thermogenesis, and neuronal excitability. When thyroid function is imbalanced—whether in hypothyroidism or hyperthyroidism—the individual experiences not only physical symptoms but alterations in mental clarity, motivation, and perception. Traditional systems have long associated sluggishness, lethargy, or restlessness with imbalance in the subtle body. It is no coincidence that these descriptions align with modern symptomatology. A hypoactive thyroid may mirror a stagnant *prāṇa*, while a hyperactive one may reflect agitated *vāta*. Thus, the alignment of thyroid hormones is not merely a medical concern—it is a spiritual imperative, ensuring that the vehicle of the body is calibrated for inner work.

Hormones also influence memory and imagination, faculties deeply entwined with spiritual experience. The stress hormone cortisol, for instance, when elevated, impairs long-term potentiation in the hippocampus, the process through which memories are consolidated. A disorganised or trauma-saturated endocrine system can impede the ability to reflect, remember, or envision—capacities essential to prayer, self-inquiry, and meditation. Conversely, balanced hormonal function enhances these faculties, making it possible to recall sacred truths, visualise divine forms, or sustain focus during extended contemplation. This is why the cultivation of inner balance is not just a moral discipline—it is cognitive preparation for the sacred.

It is also worth considering the role of hormones in the emergence of moral intuition and ethical clarity. Studies in neuroendocrinology have shown that oxytocin and vasopressin influence prosocial behaviours, trust, and empathy, suggesting that what we consider "virtue" may have hormonal correlates. Far from reducing ethics to chemistry, this observation invites a more integrated view: that virtue arises not only from cultural conditioning but from biological readiness. The saint or sage, whose presence radiates compassion and peace, is not merely acting on principle—they are biologically aligned with states of coherence, resonance, and hormonal harmony.

In this framework, the endocrine system can be seen as a bridge between will and grace. One can train the body through discipline—diet, sleep, movement, and mindfulness—but the deepest alignments often occur in surrender. This surrender, known in yogic terms as *Īśvarapraṇidhāna,* is not passivity but receptivity: a state in which the self opens to a higher intelligence, allowing neurochemical reorganisation to take place spontaneously. Many spiritual breakthroughs—sudden peace, healing, or insight—occur not through effort but through release. The body, when surrendered, becomes a lab for grace, and the hormones become its chemical testament.

Finally, we must return to the role of awareness. For in the end, it is not hormones that determine destiny, but the consciousness that witnesses them. The realised being is not free from hormonal fluctuation, but from identification with it. Hunger may arise, yet does not disturb the Self. Arousal may flicker, yet finds no fixation. Grief may swell, yet it flows through a field that remains untouched. This is the essence of spiritual maturity—not the conquest of biology, but the realisation of its transparency.

In such a one, every cell pulses with remembrance. The hormones flow as they must, serving their sacred function. And yet the being does not ride their tides—they stand on the shore, watching the waves, knowing they are neither the sea nor the storm, but the sky in which they appear.

In this knowing, hormones are no longer obstacles to transcendence—they are sacraments of embodiment, divine instruments in the symphony of form, each secretion a note in the raga of becoming. To honour them is to honour the design of creation. To align with them is to prepare the vessel. And to see through them is to discover the One who needs no chemistry to be whole.

As the final reflections of this inquiry unfold, it becomes evident that hormones are not mere mediators of physiological function—they are integral to the unfolding of human consciousness. They are part of an intricate communication system that not only sustains life but also enables the refinement of perception, the blossoming of inner stillness, and the embodiment of spiritual states. Their cycles mirror the cycles of nature; their rhythms reflect the tides of *prāṇa*; and their balance governs not only health, but the very possibility of transcendence within the human frame.

In the classical yogic traditions, the journey toward liberation—*mokṣa*—has always begun with self-regulation. The practitioner is not asked to escape the body, but to refine it. The *yamas* and *niyamas*, the ethical foundations of yoga, serve not only to promote moral development but also to foster physiological stability. Non-violence reduces adrenaline; truthfulness settles the nervous system; moderation cultivates hormonal equilibrium. Each practice is a neuroendocrine intervention, grounding the aspirant before higher states of meditation can be entered safely.

Modern science, particularly in the domains of neuroplasticity and psychoneuroimmunology, has begun to articulate a similar picture. It shows that spiritual practice shapes not only beliefs but also biological function, that repeated inner states of compassion, gratitude, and stillness reorganise the neuroendocrine system itself. Long-term meditators exhibit lower levels of inflammatory markers, reduced stress hormone profiles, and enhanced activity in the prefrontal cortex and anterior cingulate regions, which are responsible for compassion, ethical reasoning, and self-awareness.

These findings bridge the once-gulf between matter and spirit, between science and *sādhanā*. They show that the endocrine system, far from being a mechanical backdrop to spiritual life, is the alchemical interface through which spiritual life becomes embodied. Hormones thus deserve not only medical attention but reverent attention—as expressions of the sacred within the physiological.

And yet, the final truth that spiritual traditions consistently remind us of is that we are not the body. Nor are we the hormones, the glands, the thoughts, or the breath. We are the witnesses of all of these—consciousness itself. In this witness, hormones are seen not as limitations but as expressions. There are fluctuations on the surface of being, like ripples on the surface of a still lake. They are part of the dance, not the dancer.

This awareness does not negate biology; it transcends identification with it. It allows the seeker to live fully within the embodied condition while no longer being defined by it. Such a person respects the body as sacred, tends to the hormones as messengers, but remains ever-rooted in the unmoving centre of awareness.

In conclusion, the endocrine system, in all its complexity and subtlety, may be understood as the silent partner in the spiritual journey. It responds to every inner shift, is shaped by silence, and disturbed by excess. It nourishes clarity and reveals imbalance. And when aligned with the deeper intelligence of life—through meditation, right action, conscious living, and grace—it becomes the alchemy through which the soul may rise, illumined not only by philosophy but by the very chemistry of light.

Chapter 10

The Mind-Body-Spirit Continuum

The human being is not a sum of disconnected parts, but a single, sentient flow of energy, thought, form, and light. In the spiritual sciences of ancient India, this truth is axiomatic. What we call "mind," "body," and "spirit" are not separate entities but interconnected modalities of the same consciousness, expressing itself at different frequencies. This continuum is not metaphorical—it is literal, experiential, and measurable in both subtle and biological terms. The pain of grief is felt in the chest, the shock of fear reverberates in the gut, the sweetness of love warms the skin, while the clarity of insight shifts posture and breath. In every such experience, we witness a profound truth: consciousness is embodied, and the body is a vessel for the spiritual unfolding of the soul.

Modern neuroscience and ancient metaphysics converge on this insight. Research into neuroplasticity confirms that the mind, through attention and repetition, physically sculpts the brain. Psychological states alter immune function, cellular repair, and hormonal rhythms. Emotional patterns leave traces in the fascia, the viscera, and even gene expression—a field now known as epigenetics. Simultaneously, Vedic philosophy teaches that the *ātman*, the eternal Self, resides not above the body but within it, witnessing and guiding life through layers of perception, memory, and karma. Between these poles—the physical and the transcendent—exists the entire range of human experience: trauma, joy, ecstasy, sorrow, revelation. And all of it is stored in what the yogic tradition calls the *kośas*, the five sheaths of existence.

The *Annamaya Kośa*, or sheath of food, is the densest layer—the physical body made of flesh, bone, and organs. It is through this sheath that all spiritual work begins, for the body is not an obstacle to enlightenment but its foundation. In the *Taittirīya Upaniṣad*, the journey inward begins with the body. It moves through more subtle layers: the *Prāṇamaya Kośa* (vital energy), the *Manomaya Kośa* (mind), the *Vijñānamaya Kośa* (intelligence), and the *Ānandamaya Kośa* (bliss). Trauma disrupts this sequence, fracturing the continuum. When unresolved psychological pain embeds in the *Manomaya Kośa*, it influences the *Prāṇamaya* and *Annamaya* layers, manifesting as chronic tension, inflammation, or disease. Joy, on the other hand, flows freely, nourishing every sheath like sacred nectar.

In the Vedas, the recognition of this continuum is not theoretical—it is hymnal. In the Ṛgveda, the human being is addressed not as a machine or mind, but as a composite of light and will:

"यत्रा ब्रह्मा विश्वरूपाणि वेद
स वै पश्यति ब्रह्म योनिम्।"

(Yatrā brahmā viśvarūpāṇi veda
sa vai paśyati brahma yonim.)

— *Ṛgveda 1.164.39*

(Where the knower sees the manifold forms of Brahman, there he sees the womb of the Absolute.)

This recognition is the cornerstone of somatic spirituality. The body is not rejected or transcended but regarded as the yoni of Brahman, the sacred field in which the divine becomes experience. To ignore the body is to miss the very place where spiritual realisation ripens.

Modern psychological research aligns increasingly with this view. Studies on somatic memory, pioneered by clinicians such as Bessel van der Kolk and Peter Levine, demonstrate that trauma is not just a mental narrative but a bodily imprint. Events that overwhelm the nervous system—such as accidents, loss, or abuse—leave lasting residues in muscle tension, posture, breathing patterns, and autonomic dysregulation. The body, in essence, remembers what the mind may forget. These residues shape our sense of self, our capacity for trust, and our ability to access peace. Healing, therefore, must include not only talk therapy or philosophical insight, but also direct work with the body, restoring safety, rhythm, and the capacity to feel without overwhelming emotions.

In yoga, this process is known as śarīra śuddhi, the purification of the body, not as a moral act, but as a practical necessity. As the nervous system resets and prāṇa flows unimpeded, the soul regains its seat as the witness. The body, when cleansed of holding patterns, becomes a transparent medium for spiritual light. In such a state, even difficult memories cease to disturb; they remain present but no longer possess agency. They become part of the sacred biography of the Self, etched not as scars but as lines in a divine manuscript.

Emotions, too, are part of this continuum. Joy is not an abstract feeling—it is a neurohormonal cascade, involving serotonin, dopamine, endorphins, and oxytocin. These chemicals not only uplift mood but also affect immune competence, digestion, sleep, and even cellular repair. Spiritual joy, known as ānanda, goes further. It is not simply pleasure, but a state of inner resonance where every layer of the being aligns with truth. In such moments, the individual experiences not elation but equanimity, not thrill but depth. This is the bliss of the Ānandamaya Kośa—the inner body of joy, untouched by circumstance, awakened not by sensation but by remembrance of the Self.

"आनन्दो ब्रह्मेति व्यजानात्।
आनन्दाद्ध्येव खल्विमानि भूतानि जायन्ते।"

(Ānando brahmeti vyajānāt.
Ānandāddhyeva khalvimāni bhūtāni jāyante.)

— *Taittirīya Upaniṣad 3.6.1*

(He realized that bliss is Brahman. From bliss, indeed, all beings are born.)

This passage affirms that bliss is not a reward but the very origin of being. To dwell in bliss is not to attain something new, but to return to our ontological state. And the gateway to this return is not elsewhere—it is within the mind-body-spirit continuum itself.

A vibrant area of this continuum is emotional intelligence, a term popularised in modern psychology to describe the capacity to perceive, regulate, and integrate emotion. In spiritual terms, emotional intelligence is the discipline of the heart, the ability to feel deeply without being consumed, to act compassionately without losing clarity, and to witness anger or sadness without becoming identified with them. The *Bhagavad Gītā* extols this virtue:

"दुःखेष्वनुद्विग्नमनाः सुखेषु विगतस्पृहः ।
वीतरागभयक्रोधः स्थितधीर्मुनिरुच्यते ॥"

(Duḥkheṣvanudvigna-manāḥ sukheṣu vigata-spṛhaḥ
vīta-rāga-bhaya-krodhaḥ sthita-dhīr munir ucyate.)

— *Bhagavad Gītā 2.56*

(He whose mind is undisturbed by sorrow, who does not hanker after pleasure, who is free from attachment, fear, and anger—such a sage is said to be of steady wisdom.)

This is not emotional suppression but emotional mastery. It arises not through denial but through integration. The emotionally intelligent *yogi* does not negate feelings; they honour them as part of the sacred flow, allowing them to rise and fall within the stillness of awareness.

This emotional clarity reshapes the nervous system. Repeated states of presence—especially during emotionally charged experiences—strengthen the vagal tone, enhance heart rate variability, and increase activity in the insula, the brain region associated with empathy and interoception. What emerges is a person who is not only more regulated but also more embodied, more available to the sacred in each moment. They become like the ancient *ṛṣis*—sensitive, stable, surrendered.

These shifts, once thought metaphysical, are now measurable. The fields of affective neuroscience, embodied cognition, and polyvagal theory confirm what *yogis* have practised for millennia: that the body shapes the mind, that the body listens to the heart, and that the heart, when attuned, becomes a portal to the eternal.

This is why *stotras*, *mantras*, and rituals have such enduring power. They are not merely devotional—they are neurological entrainment tools. The rhythmic chanting of sacred syllables, such as the *Mahāmṛtyunjaya Mantra* or the *Śrī Rudram*, stabilises breathing, synchronises heart and brain waves, and entrains the mind to subtler frequencies of consciousness. The *Śrī Rudram*, for instance, is more than praise—it is vibrational purification, known to calm the autonomic system and deepen states of meditation. This is not speculative; EEG and HRV studies on *mantra* practitioners show consistent evidence of enhanced coherence, reduced stress markers, and greater left-right brain synchronisation.

To chant is to recalibrate. To breathe with awareness is to access the limbic brain from the diaphragm. To sit with the spine erect and the mind still is to activate the endocrine system's highest faculties, secreting not just melatonin or oxytocin, but the subtle *rasa* of consciousness itself.

What emerges from this synthesis is a vision of healing that is not symptom-focused but holistic. The broken heart affects the gut. The suppressed memory alters posture. The repressed voice tightens the throat. The unresolved fear depletes the kidneys. And yet, with every breath, every chant, every tear released in awareness, the continuum begins to reweave itself. The *kośas* align, the *nāḍīs* clear, the hormones rebalance, and the soul, no longer suffocated, rises like a flame from the body's centre.

In this space, the body becomes a temple, the breath becomes prayer, the mind becomes the altar and the spirit—the one who watches, who knows, who remembers—takes its rightful place as both pilgrim and path.

This is the truth of the mind-body-spirit continuum. It is not a concept. It is a reality waiting to be lived.

As we delve deeper into understanding the human being as a unified field of consciousness, biology, and awareness, the role of neuroplasticity becomes vital. Neuroplasticity—the brain's capacity to form and reorganise synaptic connections, especially in response to learning, experience, or trauma—is not merely a neurological fact but a spiritual opportunity. It affirms that transformation is always possible, that the inner architecture of perception and memory is not fixed but responsive. This truth is echoed in the Upanishadic assertion that the Self is neither born nor dies; still, the coverings—the impressions, identities, and behaviours—are mutable, subject to purification and refinement.

The brain, once thought to be hardwired by early adulthood, is now understood to be malleable across the lifespan. Every act of sustained attention, every practice of compassion or silence, reconfigures neural pathways. This is *sādhanā* at its deepest level—not only mental but structural. For example, mindfulness meditation, studied extensively by neuroscientists such as Richard Davidson and Sara Lazar, has been shown to increase cortical thickness in the prefrontal cortex, the seat of awareness and decision-making, while reducing volume in the amygdala, the centre of fear and emotional reactivity. What ancient *yogis* achieved through *tapas* and *dhyāna* is now being mapped through fMRI scans—evidence that conscious practice sculpts the brain toward liberation.

And yet, neuroplasticity is value-neutral. It can serve both freedom and bondage. Trauma also shapes the brain. In cases of chronic stress, neglect, or abuse, neural networks encode hypervigilance, emotional numbing, or dissociation. The body becomes a survival machine, sacrificing joy for safety. But this, too, is reversible. Through consistent inner work, such as movement, breath, mantra, and relational safety, the exact neuroplastic mechanisms allow for reconnection, regulation, and resilience. In this, we witness not only the mercy of the nervous system but its intelligence: it preserves the organism in darkness and offers renewal in light.

The Vedic seers knew this. In their profound subtlety, they offered not dogma but *mantras*, not commandments but vibration. A mantra is not merely a sound—it is a neuro-linguistic frequency, a carrier wave for intention, purification, and realignment. Each syllable, when chanted with awareness, engages the vagal system, stabilises respiration, and re-patterns mental rhythms. The *Gāyatrī Mantra*, considered the mother of all Vedic hymns, does not implore the divine—it evokes it, tuning the mind to the brilliance of the cosmic intelligence:

"ॐ भूर्भुवः स्वः।
तत्सवितुर्वरेण्यं।
भर्गो देवस्य धीमहि।
धियो यो नः प्रचोदयात्॥"

Let us meditate on the radiant source of all light. May that divine illumination awaken our intellect.

The brilliance of this *mantra* is not poetic—it is practical. Regular recitation has been shown to increase alpha brain waves, enhance memory, and induce meditative absorption. It harmonises the *manomaya kośa* (mind-body) and the *vijñānamaya kośa* (intelligence-body), paving the way for intuitive wisdom. What the ancients knew through intuition, we now glimpse through data: sound is medicine, especially when sacred.

In the continuum of healing, however, sound must be accompanied by embodiment. The spiritual aspirant cannot ascend the ladder of consciousness by bypassing the pain locked in the flesh. The wisdom of somatic experiencing, a modern therapeutic modality pioneered by Peter Levine, teaches that the nervous system heals not through stories but through felt sense, through reclaiming the body as safe territory. Similarly, *yoga nidrā*—the yogic sleep—guides the practitioner to traverse the sheaths of being, gently bringing attention to body parts, breath, emotions, and subtle energies. This practice facilitates neural integration and trauma resolution, without activating defensive systems. It is a form of deep listening, a prayer from the cells to the Self.

The Upanishads speak repeatedly of this interior listening:

"श्रवणायापि बहुभिर्यो न लभ्यः।
शृण्वन्तोऽपि बहवो यं न विद्युः।"

(He is not attained by many who hear of Him, and even when heard of, He is not known by many.)

— *Kaṭha Upaniṣad 1.2.7*

This verse reminds us that hearing the Truth is not enough. One must become quiet enough to receive it. The body must be softened, the breath regulated, the mind still. Only then does the continuum become permeable, allowing the light of the Self to infuse the being.

Love, too, is an essential part of this continuum. It is not the love of longing or attachment, but the grounded, steady warmth that opens the body and calms the mind. When one feels genuinely loved or loving, the physiological responses are unmistakable: heart rate synchronises, oxytocin rises, cortisol drops, and vagal tone increases. These changes are not merely emotional—they are sacred physiology. They reflect what mystics have called the state of grace: a condition where the body is no longer defending, the mind no longer grasping, and the soul finally resting in its radiance.

When such a state is stabilised through spiritual practice, it becomes *bhāva*—a devotional mood that infuses every perception with tenderness and awe. In the Bhakti traditions, this *bhāva* is cultivated through music, poetry, and a relationship with the divine in personal form. In *Advaita Vedānta*, the same *bhāva* emerges as pure awareness, detached yet intimate. In both cases, the continuum is respected—the body is not bypassed but saturated with presence, becoming the very fabric of devotion.

In the ultimate flowering of this path, all fragmentation dissolves. The mind no longer speaks a different language from the body. The spirit no longer floats above experience. Everything becomes One Pulse, One Presence, One Light. This is not a fantasy—it is the lived experience of the awakened ones, the *ṛṣis* and saints who walked the earth not as escapees from matter but as embodiments of clarity.

When we contemplate their lives, not just their teachings, we see a remarkable physiological coherence. Their bodies were resilient, their hearts unburdened, their eyes steady. They slept little, ate with moderation, and moved with grace. This was not a product of genetics or austerity alone. It was the refined continuum in action—a mind-body-spirit fully attuned to truth.

To walk this path is to enter the sacred laboratory of the self. It is to observe the interplay of thought and breath, of sensation and memory, of emotion and ether. It is to make the body a shrine, the mind a disciple, and the spirit the teacher.

And when this trinity is aligned, the result is not an escape from life, but an arrival into it, fully, reverently, and consciously.

The sages have long proclaimed that to know the Self is to know all. But this knowing is not intellectual; it is existential, embodied, and ever-present. It cannot be forced by willpower nor attained through the severance of form. It must arise naturally, as a river flows into the sea, through the harmonisation of mind, body, and spirit. When this continuum is respected, healed, and consciously engaged, realisation becomes not a distant goal but a natural unfolding—a remembering of what was never lost.

In modern discourse, spirituality is often seen as distinct from psychology or physiology, but this fragmentation is a cultural artefact, not a reflection of truth. The ancient Indian worldview, as well as the integrative sciences of today, affirm that the psyche is embodied, that the body is sentient, and that consciousness pervades all. Thus, trauma is not an interruption of mental peace alone—it is a disturbance in the field of presence, a fissure in the sacred web of *soma* and soul. Conversely, joy is not merely emotional—it is the signature of coherence, the music of life when every aspect of our being plays in tune.

The science of epigenetics has revealed that even our genes are not deterministic. They respond to the environment, behaviour, thought, and belief. Practices such as meditation, loving relationships, breathwork, and chanting have been shown to switch off inflammatory genes and activate those responsible for regeneration, immunity, and emotional resilience. What this means is extraordinary: that spirituality can alter biology, that insight can modify the genome, and that the soul's alignment expresses itself in flesh.

The *Upanishads*, composed in silence and received in direct realisation, confirm this truth in different languages. They teach that the Self is sat-*cit-ānanda*—existence, consciousness, and bliss, not confined to the mind, but pervading all layers of being. In the *Muṇḍaka Upaniṣad*, the seeker is advised to purify not just thought but life itself, for the truth is seen not by the confused or conflicted, but by the one whose inner and outer are reconciled:

**"यस्य नाहंकारो न ममता न किञ्चित्
तमेव शान्तं ब्रह्मविदां वदन्ति।"**

(He in whom there is no ego, no possessiveness, he alone is peaceful, and the knower of Brahman.)

In this silence of self-making, the continuum reweaves itself. The mind ceases its compulsive narration, and the body releases its defences. The spirit, no longer occluded, becomes the guiding flame. The individual begins to live not from fragmentation but from wholeness, not from history but from presence.

This is not a mystical ideal—it is a physiological and spiritual reality. It can be felt in the quality of breath, in the stillness of gaze, in the warmth of the heart. It can be heard in the depth of the *mantra "So'ham"*—I am that—not as a claim but as a recognition. The voice that once shouted "I" begins to whisper "All."

In the *Śiva Sutras*, a profound text from the Kashmir Śaiva tradition, this realisation is captured with stunning brevity:

"चित्तं मन्त्रः।"

(The mind itself is mantra.)

When this is known, all divisions collapse. The *mantra* is not separate from thought, thought is not separate from flesh, flesh is not separate from the soul, and the soul is not separate from the Source.

Thus, the mind-body-spirit continuum is not something to be created—it is something to be uncovered. Beneath the layers of conditioning, trauma, and cultural fragmentation, this unity waits, pulsing gently, calling us home. The practices of *yoga*, the insights of psychology, the gifts of science, and the revelations of scripture are not separate paths but complementary approaches to the same sacred end: to remember that we are whole, that we have always been whole, and that to live from this wholeness is to become a light unto the world.

When this realisation dawns, healing is no longer a project—it is a side-effect of truth. Enlightenment is no longer a peak—it is the natural rhythm of being aligned. The body becomes a shrine not by denying it, but by infusing it with presence. The mind becomes sacred not by silencing it, but by training it to reflect the real. The spirit is not far—it is the substance of all appearance.

And so, the final instruction, whispered across centuries by sages and scientists alike, is this: Return. Return not to a doctrine or dogma, but to the body as it breathes, to the mind as it listens, to the spirit as it reveals. Return to the place where trauma is held and released, where love is felt and offered, where silence is heard and lived. Return to the continuum—and know that it has always been you.

Chapter 11

Breathe – The Invisible Guide

In the quiet rise and fall of breath lies one of the greatest mysteries of human existence. It is constant, yet unnoticed; essential, yet so subtle that we often forget it altogether. Yet, within this quiet rhythm, is hidden the key to self-mastery, to healing, to inner peace, and even to enlightenment. Breath is not just a biological function—it is the bridge between body and consciousness, the sacred rhythm that links the outer world of form to the inner world of stillness. To breathe with awareness is to begin a journey inward, a journey that has been described in scriptures, refined by *yogis*, measured by scientists, and honoured by mystics across traditions.

In Sanskrit, the word for breath is *prāṇa*, which means much more than air. *Prāṇa* is life-force, the intelligent energy that animates all existence. It is present in the inhale and exhale, in the wind, in sunlight, in thought, and in the silent presence that underlies all action. In the *Upaniṣads*, *prāṇa* is described not merely as a physiological agent but as the foundation of life itself:

"प्राणो हि जीवः।"

(Prāṇo hi jīvaḥ.)

— *Chāndogya Upaniṣad*

(Prāṇa is indeed life.)

This statement is not metaphorical. In both ancient understanding and modern science, breath reflects the quality of life. When we are calm, the breath slows and deepens. When we are anxious or afraid, it becomes shallow and rapid. Each emotion and thought alters the breath. But more importantly, each conscious adjustment of breath can alter emotion, thought, and even hormonal and neural function. It is this bidirectional power that makes breath the invisible guide, the sovereign tool for self-regulation and awakening.

The physiological basis for this is now well-established. Breathing is governed by both autonomic and voluntary systems, meaning it can be automatic or consciously controlled. This dual function enables it to serve as a bridge between unconscious processes (such as heart rate and hormone secretion) and conscious states (such as focus and stillness). When we engage the breath intentionally, we send signals through the vagus nerve, which modulates the parasympathetic nervous system, thereby reducing cortisol levels, lowering heart rate, and enhancing digestion, repair, and immune resilience. In contrast, disordered or rapid breathing can activate the sympathetic nervous system, fueling stress and disconnection.

This understanding was intuitively known to *yogis*, who developed a detailed science of breath called *prāṇāyāma*—the expansion and regulation of *prāṇa* through specific techniques. The *Haṭha Yoga Pradīpikā*, an essential text on yogic practice, declares:

"चले वाते चलं चित्तं निश्चले निश्चलं भवेत्।"

(When the breath moves, the mind moves. When the breath is still, the mind is still.)

This profound observation underscores that breath is the key to mental clarity and stillness. Practices such as *nāḍī śodhana* (alternate nostril breathing), *kapālabhāti* (cleansing breath), *bhastrikā* (bellows breath), and *sūrya bhedana* (right nostril breath) are designed not merely for health, but to refine perception, cleanse karmic residues, and prepare the mind for deep meditation. Each of these techniques affects the nervous system in unique ways—balancing hemispheric brain activity, oxygenating tissues, enhancing cerebral circulation, and promoting alpha and theta brainwave states associated with inner stillness.

Beyond their physical benefits, these practices induce shifts in consciousness. Regular *prāṇāyāma* changes one's sense of time, identity, and separateness. Breath becomes a vehicle of transcendence, revealing that the mind is not a fixed entity but a process dependent on rhythm, attention, and flow. In this sense, the breath is a *mantra* without words, a movement through which awareness touches its source.

Modern forms of breathwork, such as holotropic breathing, rebirthing breathwork, and conscious connected breathing, have extended these insights into therapeutic settings. Developed by pioneers like Dr. Stanislav Grof, these techniques induce non-ordinary states of consciousness through prolonged rhythmic breathing, often accompanied by music and bodywork. Participants frequently report emotional release, insights into early life trauma, spiritual experiences, and states of oneness. Neurobiologically, such practices alter CO_2 and O_2 ratios, stimulating areas of the brain involved in memory, emotion, and interoception. But more than chemistry, it is the intimacy with breath—and thus with the Self—that catalyses healing. Mystical traditions across the world have recognised this. In Sufism, breath is the essence of *dhikr*, or remembrance. In *Taoist alchemy*, the breath is cultivated to circulate energy through the microcosmic orbit. In *Christian hesychasm*, the Jesus Prayer is synchronised with the rhythm of inhalation and exhalation, gradually drawing the practitioner into stillness and union. Across these paths, the breath is not merely functional—it is sacred, a sacrament of the present moment, a pulse of the divine within the ephemeral body.

In moments of profound meditation, or spontaneous mystical absorption, breath behaves in mysterious ways. It may slow to a whisper, almost disappearing, or it may pause altogether in a state known as *kevala kumbhaka*—spontaneous breath retention. *Yogis* and saints have spoken of these states as *samādhi*, where the external world recedes and the self dissolves into pure awareness. These are not physiological anomalies; they are the signatures of spiritual stillness, when the life-force no longer needs movement to know itself. Scientific studies on advanced meditators have recorded unusual metabolic and respiratory patterns, including decreased oxygen consumption, increased coherence across brain regions, and altered gamma-wave activity—all markers of heightened states of integration.

Yet, the invitation of the breath is not reserved for the advanced. Every human, in every moment, carries within them the same access point. Each inhale is an invitation to arrive, and each exhale is a chance to release. The breath asks only one thing: that we notice it. For in that noticing, the spiral of thought slows, the heart softens, the body realigns, and the spirit begins to speak without sound.

Breath also reflects truth. It does not lie. We can smile while grieving, speak calmly while angry, perform tasks while anxious—but the breath reveals our inner state. It tightens, shortens, and escapes rhythm. And when healing begins, it is first felt in the breath. A sigh, a deep inhale, a long exhale—these are signs of the soul returning home. They are physiological, but they are also spiritual movements, gateways through which presence re-enters the temple of the body.

Thus, to master the breath is not to dominate it, but to befriend it. It is to recognise breath as the *guru*, the witness, the companion that has never left. From the first gasp of life to the final release, it is breath that accompanies us, measures our days, and, if we allow, guides our awakening.

In the Vedas, *prāṇa* is invoked not only as life-force but as sacred deity:

"प्राणो अग्निः प्राणः सूर्यः प्राणो वायुः।
प्राणं धीयं प्रजापतिः प्रजापतिर्भवति।"

(Prāṇa is Agni. Prāṇa is Sūrya. Prāṇa is Vāyu.
Prāṇa is the intellect. Prāṇa is Prajāpati, the lord of all beings.)

— *Praśna Upaniṣad*

In this exaltation, we glimpse the ancient awe reserved for breath. It is not mere air. It is the divine guest, moving silently through the corridors of flesh and thought. To ignore it is to remain asleep. To honour it is to begin the ascent—not away from the world, but into its very heart, where breath and spirit are revealed to be the same.

To live in alignment with breath is to live in alignment with truth. It is not the abstract truth of beliefs or doctrines, but the embodied truth of what is—now, here, without distortion. When the breath flows freely, the nervous system relaxes into a state of co-regulation, the heart finds coherence, the digestive system resumes its rhythm, and the brain slips into alpha states of peaceful alertness. This coherence is not an accident; it is the result of listening. For the breath teaches what no scripture can fully capture: the art of being.

This coherence is also relational. Breath is not only personal—it is inter-subjective. In close relationships, research shows that the breathing patterns of people can synchronise, a phenomenon known as physiological entrainment. Mothers and infants breathe in synchrony during moments of attunement. Lovers, meditators in group settings, even teachers and students during *satsang*, can find their breath spontaneously aligning. This resonance is not symbolic—it is real, a mirror of shared presence. In spiritual traditions, this synchrony becomes a field through which energy, silence, and even insight are transmitted. A *Guru's* mere presence can alter a disciple's breathing rhythm, shifting them into calm, receptive states. This is why breath, in its most refined form, becomes not just a personal practice but a portal to collective awareness.

Breath also guides emotional processing. Every emotion has a unique breath signature. Anger shortens and sharpens the breath, anxiety makes it erratic and shallow, depression flattens it, joy opens it up, and gratitude softens it. These patterns are not fixed; they are changeable through awareness. By consciously altering our breath—lengthening the exhale, slowing the pace, or pausing at the top or bottom—we create space for new emotional tones to emerge. Breath becomes a modulator of emotion, a sovereign act of inner choice. This is the heart of spiritual maturity: the ability to remain spacious amidst sensation, to respond rather than react, to breathe and then act, rather than act and then regret.

At deeper levels of practice, breath becomes the object of meditative absorption. In *ānāpānasati*, the Buddha taught mindfulness of breathing as the direct path to liberation. This simple yet profound practice involves observing the natural breath as it enters and exits the nostrils, without interference. Over time, the mind grows still, and the observer and the observed begin to merge. The breath, once a physical sensation, becomes a vortex into spacious awareness. Many advanced meditators report that in these states, the breath becomes so subtle that it is barely perceptible. Yet awareness sharpens—not into effort, but into presence without boundary.

In the yogic system, breath is intimately connected to the subtle energy channels, or *nāḍīs*. Of the 72,000 *nāḍīs* described, the three primary ones—*iḍā*, *piṅgalā*, and *suṣumnā*—run along the spinal axis. *Iḍā* is associated with the left nostril, being lunar, cooling, and feminine. *Piṅgalā* is associated with the right nostril, being solar, warming, and masculine. *Suṣumnā*, the central channel, is dormant until *prāṇa* is balanced. Once activated, it becomes the pathway of awakening, allowing *kuṇḍalinī* to rise and unite the practitioner with the supreme consciousness. Breath is the key to this activation. Through *nāḍī śodhana* (alternate nostril breathing) and *kumbhaka* (breath retention), these channels are purified and awakened.

Yet, this path is not mechanical; it is devotional. The breath must be approached not as a technique alone, but as a sacred offering. In many *Tantric* texts, *prāṇa* is called *havis*—offering.

Each inhale is an acceptance, and each exhale is a surrender. When this attitude permeates breathwork, the practice becomes *pūjā*, an inner ritual through which the divine is both offered and received.

This sacredness extends to the breath's relationship with *mantra.* The ancient formula *"So'ham"*—meaning "I am that"—arises naturally in conjunction with the breath. "So" with the inhale and "Ham" with the exhale. It is not chanted; it is heard. The *yogis* listen to the breath as they chant this eternal truth, and in that listening, identification with the ego falls away. The breath reveals what the mind cannot: the Self as universal, the moment as whole, and the body as temple.

In mystical states, this awareness can deepen into non-dual absorption. Here, the practitioner no longer breathes intentionally, nor even observes the breath as "mine." The breath breathes itself, the body sits without volition, and thought ceases without force. The "I" dissolves into spacious witnessing, where nothing needs to be added, changed, or improved. This is not passivity—it is radical inclusion, where even pain or noise is seen as part of the breath's dance. This is *samādhi* not as escape, but as fullness.

And yet, the breath also grounds. After peak experiences, it is the breath that brings the mystic back into the body, back into human relationships, back into service. The breath does not abandon the world. It transforms the one who walks through it. A person who has trained their breath becomes a person of presence—steady, warm, resilient, available. They speak less, but with weight. They move slowly, but with clarity. Their calm becomes a blessing, not through effort, but through inner coherence that the breath has taught.

Thus, to live with the breath as a guide is to live in truth. It is to walk this world not with tension but with grace, not with reactivity but with rhythm. The breath becomes the teacher that asks no questions and gives no commands; it simply reminds: come back, begin again, receive, let go.

And in this remembering, one realises: breath is not just the path. It is the presence of the sacred itself, moving through lungs and ribs and silence. It is invisible, but it leaves its signature on everything. A life attuned to breath is a life attuned to peace—not the peace of withdrawal, but the peace that arises when all things are welcomed, and the Self is known as the one who breathes them all into being.

In the end, what breath offers is more than technique, more than relaxation, more than focus. It offers return to the Self, to stillness, to the essence from which all action arises. This is why every spiritual tradition, no matter how diverse in doctrine, eventually finds its way back to the breath. In the breath, the mystic sees not only survival, but spiritus—the Latin root of both "spirit" and "breath." In the exhalation, we meet surrender. In the inhalation, we meet renewal. And between the two, in that sacred pause, we touch the infinite silence of Being.

From the first gasp that initiates life to the final exhale that marks its end, breath is our most faithful companion. Unlike thought, it does not judge; unlike emotion, it does not cling; unlike identity, it does not defend. It flows in the presence of fear and the wake of joy. It witnesses both trauma and transformation. And it asks for nothing—only that we remember it, only that we allow it to guide us home.

In yogic cosmology, the final breath is not a tragedy but a transition. The *Bṛhadāraṇyaka Upaniṣad* tells us that as *prāṇa* leaves the body, it does not disappear—it returns to the cosmic whole from which it arose. The individual breath, long identified as "mine," is revealed as never having been separate; it was borrowed starlight, entrusted for a while, and now exhaled into the timeless womb of creation. The true *yogi* prepares for this exhale not in fear but in intimacy, for it is not a loss—it is a release into that which was always holding us.

"यदा प्राणो व्युत्क्रामति तदामनसो मनः।"
(When prāṇa departs, the mind returns to its source.)
— *Bṛhadāraṇyaka Upaniṣad 4.4.2*

Thus, the mastery of breath is the mastery of life itself. And yet, paradoxically, true mastery is not control—it is surrender, not manipulating the breath, but listening to it, not forcing stillness, but discovering the stillness that was always present behind the rise and fall.

When we live like this—breathing not just to survive, but to awaken—each moment becomes sacred. The inhale becomes a prayer, and the exhale, a blessing. Breath opens the gates of compassion, softens the hard edge of thought, and cleanses the accumulated dust of days and decades. In moments of pain, it anchors us; in moments of joy, it expands us; and in moments of meditation, it dissolves us.

There is no *Guru* greater than breath, no text is more direct, and no technique is more available. It is with us in joy, in grief, in conflict, and communion. It is here now, asking nothing, offering everything. To follow the breath is to follow the pathless path, the way of return. For in its rise and fall is written the oldest mantra: I am. I was. I will be. I am.

And so, in the end, when words fall away and forms dissolve, the seeker becomes the seer, the breath becomes the light, and the Self—silent, full, awake—remains, not as something separate, but as the very air of consciousness, the very pulse of eternity, inhaling the world, exhaling the soul, and resting always in that which neither comes nor goes.

Chapter 12

Silence, Stillness, and the Inner Sense

In a world saturated with sound, movement, and endless stimulation, silence is often mistaken for emptiness. Yet in the ancient traditions of self-realisation, silence is not absence—it is presence in its purest form. It is not a lack of speech, but a depth of listening. It is not loneliness, but a fullness that cannot be disturbed. Silence is where the mind finally lets go of its grip, where the senses no longer pull outward, and where the soul begins to whisper truths too subtle for language. In this sanctuary of stillness, one rediscovers the inner sense, the refined faculty of perception that remains when all external inputs cease.

The practice of entering silence is not a rejection of the world—it is a return to one's source. In yogic philosophy, this return is mapped through the discipline of *pratyāhāra*, the withdrawal of the senses. It is the fifth limb of the eightfold path of *yoga*, serving as a bridge between outer discipline and inner absorption. Through *pratyāhāra*, the practitioner consciously turns the energy of attention inward, away from noise, distraction, and form, and into the field of inner awareness. This is not repression but refinement. It is the moment the senses are no longer reactive instruments but offerings of awareness themselves.

Modern neuroscience supports what ancient sages long intuited. In silence and solitude, the default mode network of the brain becomes active—a system associated with self-referential thought, introspection, and memory processing. While often associated with mind-wandering, this network, when engaged consciously through meditation, becomes a portal for self-integration. Functional MRI studies have shown that long-term meditators exhibit more efficient activity in this network, resulting in a greater capacity for insight, self-awareness, and emotional balance. In silence, the brain does not go dormant—it reorganises, listens, and repairs.

Stillness, too, is misunderstood in modern life. It is often equated with passivity or idleness. But true stillness is not the absence of action—it is the ground of being beneath all action. It is the silence beneath speech, the presence beneath personality. The body may sit in stillness, but this posture becomes a mirror in which the restlessness of the mind is revealed. With practice, even this restlessness quiets, like ripples settling on a pond. And in that clarity, the seeker begins to see—not with the outer eye, but with the inner sense that perceives not form, but essence.

Meditation, when practised with depth, becomes the art of abiding in this stillness without demand. It is not a technique but a way of entering into intimacy with reality. There is no goal but to be—fully, honestly, vulnerably—with what is. Whether breath, body, sound, or silence, the object of meditation eventually dissolves, leaving only pure awareness. This awareness does not judge or compare. It simply rests. And in this resting, the mind is no longer split between past and future. It becomes unified, and the heart opens to the timeless now.

Solitude plays an essential role in this process. To be alone is not necessarily to be isolated. Solitude, when chosen and embraced, becomes a space of healing, of recalibration. It is the ground where the soul rediscovers its independence from noise and validation. In solitude, there is no one to impress, no performance to maintain, no comparison to measure. The ego has nothing to feed on. And slowly, as the external masks fall away, the inner voice becomes clear, quiet and precise. It speaks not in words, but in presence. It asks not for answers, but for honesty.

Many mystical traditions understand that prolonged silence, when coupled with inner stillness, can lead to profound openings. Saints, monks, *yogis*, and sages have entered caves, forests, deserts, and cells—not to escape life, but to meet it fully. In these places, without distraction or comfort, the surface self dissolves. The emotional tides rise and fall, and the fears and fantasies exhaust themselves. And then, what remains is not nothingness, but spaciousness—a silent, vibrant field in which the self and the divine are no longer two.

Contemporary psychology is beginning to rediscover the value of such experiences. Practices like sensory deprivation therapy, silent retreats, and meditative protocols are being studied for their impact on stress reduction, emotional regulation, and cognitive renewal. Individuals who spend even brief periods in silence often report increased clarity, improved decision-making, and heightened creativity. These are not side effects—they are the fruits of returning to the source. When the noise outside dims, the intelligence within becomes audible.

Yet silence is not always easy. It confronts us with everything we have avoided. In silence, there is no distraction from old pain, no filter for self-doubt, no escape from anxiety. This is why the path into stillness requires courage. One must be willing to face the inner landscape without sedation or distortion. But as the practice deepens, what first felt like emptiness is revealed as fullness. The sadness becomes tenderness, the fear becomes clarity, and the longing becomes love.

And at the core of it all lies the inner sense—a perceptual faculty that does not rely on eyes, ears, or intellect. It is the capacity to know without analysing, to feel without reacting, to be without effort. It is the presence behind perception, the subtle awareness that persists even in deep sleep or profound stillness. In some traditions, this is referred to as the witness, while in others, it is called the soul. Regardless of name, it is the same:

the undisturbed centre around which all experiences arise and dissolve.

When silence is no longer feared but welcomed, the entire life begins to change — Speech becomes more intentional, listening becomes more sensitive, and movement becomes more graceful. The body, once pulled by habit and tension, begins to reflect inner economy and elegance. The mind, no longer frantic for novelty, rests in presence. The heart, freed from performing, begins to be with what is.

Silence, then, is not a retreat from the world. It is a deeper entry into its sacredness. Stillness is not a delay of life's purpose—it is its foundation. And the inner sense is not a mysterious sixth faculty—it is the original one, the first echo of awareness itself, from which all others arise.

Those who dwell in silence are not empty; they are complete with presence; they are attuned, not aloof; they carry a depth that cannot be taught, only felt; their eyes are steady, and their words are rare but precise; their presence calms, not because of effort, but because they are in harmony with the unseen; they have touched the axis of being and live from that axis, not moved by praise or blame, gain or loss.

In the end, silence is not a state to achieve; it is the natural state beneath all striving. Stillness is not something to create; it is the ground of our existence, and the inner sense is not a mystical faculty; it is the truth of what we are, available always, remembered in moments of surrender, rediscovered each time we dare to stop, listen, and be. As the inner sense becomes more finely attuned, a transformation begins that cannot be reversed. The individual starts to experience silence not as something entered or left, but as a background field that is always present—beneath sound, beneath thought, even beneath emotion. It is discovered that silence is not the absence of life but its substrate. Everything rises from it and returns to it, like waves from an ocean. This is not a philosophical abstraction—it is a lived perception, cultivated through inner discipline and refined attention. The more one abides in this silent field, the more it begins to shape the very structure of identity.

In daily life, this results in a subtle but profound reorientation. The reactive tendencies of the mind soften, and the hunger for stimulation fades. Situations that once provoked strong emotional reactions are now met with clarity and a sense of spaciousness. This is not suppression but freedom. The individual is no longer pulled unconsciously into every external fluctuation because there is an anchor within—a still point, untouched by circumstance. This still point is what mystics have referred to as the centre, the axis, or the seat of being. In neuroscience, such inner stability is correlated with increased parasympathetic tone, decreased activity in the amygdala, and enhanced connectivity in the prefrontal cortex. In other words, spiritual stillness maps to neurophysiological resilience.

Silence also sharpens discernment. In the absence of noise, both internal and external, decisions are no longer driven by urgency or conditioning; they emerge from a space of profound clarity. One begins to live not reactively, but responsively. Intuition strengthens, and insight flows without strain. This is not magical thinking but the result of a nervous system that is no longer dominated by survival responses. In silence, the brain reorganises itself toward balance, not threat. From this balance comes wisdom, and from wisdom comes compassion.

Compassion is, in fact, one of the most natural fruits of silence. When the chatter of judgement quiets, when the urgency to fix or defend dissolves, what remains is a seeing that is unarmoured and open. The silent mind is not indifferent but profoundly sensitive. It feels the suffering of others without collapsing into it, and it offers presence without an agenda. It becomes a mirror in which others can recognise their stillness, their truth. In this way, silence becomes not only a personal practice but a form of service.

It is also a form of healing. Many contemporary trauma therapies emphasise the importance of creating safety in the body before processing emotional pain. Silence provides this safety, not as isolation, but as a form of containment. In silence, the unresolved parts of the psyche can surface without being overwhelmed. There is room to feel, to grieve, to witness, without the need to explain or justify. And because there is no performance, no pressure, the healing that occurs in silence is often deeper than any external intervention can achieve. It is organic, arising from the innate intelligence of the body and soul when given the space to unwind.

This space also allows for a different relationship with time. In stillness, the linear structure of time softens: the past no longer dominates, the future no longer pulls, the present expands, moments stretch out, and experience deepens. One begins to live in a different tempo, guided not by clocks or calendars, but by presence. Tasks are completed with attention, and conversations are conducted with listening. Movement becomes ritual. Life slows down, not because of lethargy, but because of reverence.

This reverence extends to all aspects of life. The silent person begins to feel the sacred in the mundane: the sound of wind through leaves, the weight of the body in a chair, the breath rising and falling—these are no longer mere background details; they become gateways into the eternal, as the division between sacred and secular dissolves. Every act becomes part of a larger ritual, and every place becomes part of the inner temple.

Yet none of this is achieved through force. The path of silence is not a strategy. It is a surrender. It is not about becoming someone different. It is about becoming no one, and in that no-one-ness, discovering the fullness of being. The mind ceases to strive, and the heart ceases to seek. And what is revealed is not a new identity, but a spaciousness in which all identities arise and fall without conflict.

Such silence cannot be contained by practices alone. It must eventually become a way of living. One may sit in meditation, walk in nature, speak with others, or even engage in worldly responsibilities, yet the silence remains. It is not dependent on the environment or activity. It is a quality of attention, a depth of presence, a quiet knowing that runs beneath all appearances. This is the ultimate expression of spiritual maturity—not withdrawal from the world, but the ability to carry the stillness of the inner sanctuary into every corner of life.

In this final understanding, silence is no longer something to do; it is something to be; it is the natural state of the awakened heart and the clear mind, the echo of the source, still vibrating beneath the forms and stories we inhabit. And to live from this silence is to live from the centre of all things, to act without tension, to speak with weight, and to move through the world as a presence that reminds others of their depth.

The world needs this silence, not as absence, but as wisdom, not as retreat, but as presence that listens before it speaks, that holds before it heals, that sees before it judges. In this way, the silent one becomes not invisible, but radiant, not withdrawn, but grounded. And through them, the world hears once again the music that only stillness can play—the music of the soul, resonating not in sound, but in the unstruck note of awareness itself.

Chapter 13

When the Body Becomes the Prayer

There comes a point on the path when the seeker no longer asks to leave the world behind but begins to see the world itself as sacred. When the disciplines of breath, silence, attention, and inner refinement ripen into presence, the senses do not become a distraction; instead, they become the very gateway to the divine. Touch is no longer mere sensation; it becomes transmission. Sight is no longer confined to form; it beholds the essence. Sound ceases to be noise; it becomes vibration. Smell and taste, once dismissed as pleasures or temptations, become direct channels into memory, devotion, and stillness. In this way, the entire body becomes an altar, and the movements of daily life—the act of walking, cooking, bathing, embracing—become the rituals of a living prayer.

This is not a metaphor. It is not the romanticisation of the mundane. It is a profound realisation born of the truth that the soul is not separate from embodiment, that the divine is not opposed to the physical, and that to live fully in one's flesh with reverence is to touch what is eternal. The body is not a distraction from the spiritual path—it is the vehicle of its revelation.

Spiritual traditions across time have wrestled with the tension between transcendence and immanence. In early asceticism, the body was often seen as a hindrance—a source of temptation, illusion, or limitation. Yet in the more integrated lineages, especially those rooted in *Tantra*, mysticism, and embodied wisdom, the body is not rejected but redeemed. It is not an enemy to be subdued, but a temple to be inhabited —an instrument tuned to the frequencies of the sacred.

To live this way is to approach each day with a sense of devotion that is not confined to formal rituals but is woven into the ordinary fabric of being. To eat with attention is to remember that food is earth transformed by light, water, fire, and human effort—a sacrament. To walk barefoot is to remember that the ground beneath us is not inert but alive. To bathe is not only to cleanse the skin but to return the body to a fluid, receptive state. These are not practices in addition to life. They are life, seen through the eye of reverence.

When the senses are refined—not indulged or denied, but sanctified—they begin to guide us toward the present moment. They no longer serve the ego's hunger for stimulation, but the soul's longing for unity. A sound heard with full presence becomes music, even if it is silence. A touch offered with intention becomes a blessing, even if it is brief. A gaze held in sincerity becomes communion, even if it is wordless. In this way, the sacred becomes tangible—not in far-off temples, but in the immediacy of embodied life.

Mindful living is the natural extension of this reverence. It is not merely awareness of thoughts or tasks—it is the full inhabitation of each moment with heart and clarity. It is the capacity to meet life not from habit, but from presence, to rise in the morning not with urgency, but with a breath of gratitude, to dress not in a rush, but in awareness of touch and texture, to speak not to fill space, but to offer something tangible. This mindfulness is not a skill to master; it is a devotion to reality as it is, without embellishment or escape.

Such mindfulness requires embodiment, not abstraction. It is not a flight into ideas or ideals but a descent into form. The spiritual path is often seen as upward, but the deeper movement is inward and downward—into the ground, into the flesh, into the heartbeat and the breath. This descent is not regression—it is integration. It is the soul entering the body fully, not to be imprisoned but to be expressed.

When this embodiment deepens, the line between inner and outer begins to blur. The sacred is no longer an experience sought in rarefied spaces; it is the scent of rain, the warmth of the sun on skin, the sound of a loved one's voice, and the ache in the chest after a heartfelt goodbye. Nothing is excluded; pain is not denied, and beauty is not clung to. Each becomes part of a greater whole—the liturgy of human life, played out through the symphony of the senses.

In this realisation, every gesture becomes a *mudrā*, every breath becomes a *mantra*, and every step becomes a pilgrimage. The body walks through the world not as a machine of consumption but as a vessel of meaning. It begins to communicate something more profound, not through words but through its very way of being. There is a softness in the eyes, a steadiness in the spine, a groundedness in the feet. These are the signs of a soul inhabiting its form, not in resistance, but in harmony.

And then, without warning, the ordinary becomes luminous. A sip of water reveals the sky. A shared glance reveals the Self. The body, so often objectified or ignored, becomes the very place where the infinite meets the intimate. It becomes not only the container of life but its expression, a prayer spoken without language, a poem of skin, breath, and bone.

This is not an ideal to chase but a truth to remember. It is not an achievement, but a homecoming. It is the natural state of those who have returned to the wisdom of the senses, to the silence beneath speech, to the stillness within movement. They are neither ascetics nor hedonists. They are simply those who have seen through the illusion of separation and now live as the thread that unites matter and meaning.

To honour the body in this way is not self-indulgence; it is self-offering. It is to treat the body as worthy of care, not because it conforms to a standard, but because it is the living presence of the divine in form. It is to move, eat, rest, and relate not out of compulsion, but in attunement. It is to live prayer not as recitation, but as embodiment.

And perhaps this is the final teaching—not that we must go somewhere else to find the sacred, but that we must come home to where we already are - in this moment, in this breath, in this body because when the senses have been purified by presence, when the mind has been tempered by stillness, and when the soul has descended into flesh with tenderness and clarity, the body itself becomes the prayer, and the world, no longer something to escape or improve, becomes the altar.

Chapter 14

The Science of Transcendence

For millennia, human beings have reported experiences that defy the boundaries of the ordinary mind—visions of radiant light, profound unity with all life, encounters with the divine, and states of blissful stillness beyond time and identity. These moments, often referred to as mystical or transcendental, have traditionally been associated with the domain of saints, sages, poets, and mystics. But as the sciences of the brain and body advance, something remarkable is becoming clear: these experiences, far from being delusions or metaphorical exaggerations, correspond to measurable changes in the nervous system, brain activity, and biochemistry. In other words, the mystical is not an escape from reality—it may be a deeper immersion into it.

This realisation is transforming the dialogue between science and spirituality. Where once there was scepticism or dismissal, there is now rigorous inquiry. Neuroscientists are mapping the meditative brain, psychologists are studying the long-term effects of non-ordinary states of consciousness, and physicians are investigating how deep states of prayer and presence influence immunity, stress response, and healing. Spirituality is no longer considered outside the scope of science. It is now seen as a dimension of human experience with physiological correlates and psychological consequences.

One of the earliest and most influential figures in this space was William James, often referred to as the father of American psychology. In his 1902 classic *The Varieties of Religious Experience,* James proposed that mystical states were not pathological, but elevated forms of consciousness that offered genuine insight. He described them as states of unity, timelessness, and ineffability—difficult to express in words, but profoundly transformative. What made these experiences credible, he argued, was their fruits: a profound and lasting change in character, compassion, and perception.

This insight has since been echoed by decades of research. Beginning in the 1960s, EEG and neuroimaging studies began to examine the brains of advanced meditators. A consistent finding was the appearance of alpha and theta brainwaves—patterns associated with calm, deep focus, and creativity. In more advanced states, gamma waves—linked to heightened awareness and integration—were observed, particularly in Tibetan monks and experienced *yogis.* These findings suggest that mystical states are not chaotic or hallucinatory; on the contrary, they are characterised by coherence, harmony, and neural synchronisation.

One landmark study, led by Richard Davidson at the University of Wisconsin, examined the brains of Buddhist monks engaged in compassion meditation. The results showed unusually high levels of gamma wave activity and heightened connectivity between regions associated with empathy and attention. The monks, many of whom had practised for over 10,000 hours, exhibited neural markers far beyond those of novice meditators. This suggests that spiritual states can be trained and that the brain adapts structurally to prolonged inner attention.

Another key area of research has emerged from the field of transpersonal psychology, founded by Abraham Maslow and Stanislav Grof. Maslow proposed that beyond basic needs and ego development lies a human potential for peak experiences—moments of awe, unity, and self-transcendence. Grof, through his work with altered states induced by breathwork and psychedelics, found that individuals consistently reported encounters with archetypal realms, past life memories, and experiences of cosmic unity. Instead of dismissing these as fantasy, Grof proposed a cartography of consciousness that included these dimensions as real, accessible, and deeply healing.

Modern psychedelic research, once halted by stigma and politics, has reemerged with scientific rigour. Institutions such as Johns Hopkins University, Imperial College London, and MAPS (Multidisciplinary Association for Psychedelic Studies) have documented how substances like psilocybin, LSD, and DMT can induce states remarkably similar to those described in mystical literature. In controlled settings, these substances can temporarily dissolve the default mode network—the brain system associated with ego and narrative identity—leading to experiences of ego dissolution, timelessness, and interconnectedness. Subjects often report these as among the most meaningful events of their lives, with long-term reductions in depression, anxiety, and existential distress. Importantly, these findings do not suggest that transcendence requires pharmacological induction. Instead, they confirm that the brain is capable of entering profoundly altered states of perception, whether through breath, meditation, sound, prayer, or movement. They validate the testimony of yogis, shamans, monks, and mystics throughout history. What was once seen as esoteric is now being mapped, quantified, and respected.

Beyond neuroscience, physiology also reveals the truth of transcendence. When individuals enter deep meditative or prayerful states, a cascade of biological changes occurs. Heart rate variability increases, indicating enhanced adaptability and parasympathetic activation. Cortisol and adrenaline levels decrease, while hormones associated with bonding and healing, such as oxytocin and serotonin, rise. The immune system functions more efficiently, inflammation markers decrease, and the ageing process slows at the cellular level. These are not minor effects. They suggest that states of inner coherence and spiritual openness optimise the body for repair, resilience, and longevity.

Even genetics is entering the conversation. The emerging science of epigenetics shows that gene expression is influenced by environment, behaviour, and mental states. Meditation, for instance, has been shown to activate genes responsible for healing and deactivate those associated with stress and disease. This means that our spiritual practices are not merely psychological—they are biochemical, reshaping the very expression of our DNA in real time.

But science is not only validating transcendence—it is being transformed by it. As researchers encounter phenomena that challenge the boundaries of reductionism, a more integrative model is emerging—one that honours both data and depth, both measurement and meaning. This model acknowledges that the universe may not be a machine. Still, a living field of intelligence and human consciousness may be both a receiver and a participant in this field.

Across cultures, this view has been expressed in diverse but resonant ways. In Hindu *Vedānta*, the world is not inert matter, but *Brahman*, the consciousness that appears as form. In Taoism, the Tao is the flowing intelligence behind all phenomena. In Indigenous cosmologies, nature is alive, aware, and sacred. And in the language of modern physics, the observer is not separate from the observed. These are not merely poetic metaphors; they point to a non-dual ontology, where mind and matter are not opposites, but expressions of one indivisible reality.

Such an understanding invites humility, reminding us that the pinnacle of knowledge is not certainty but wonder—a sense of openness to what is beyond comprehension. It suggests that the highest form of intelligence is not control, but alignment with that which is greater than the self. In this space, science becomes a tool not of dominance, but of reverence; spirituality becomes not belief, but direct knowing, and the human being is revealed not as a spectator in the cosmos, but as a node of consciousness, capable of tuning into the subtle harmonics of the whole.

This is the science of transcendence—not a science of escape, but a science of return. It brings us back to what the mystics have always known: that truth is not somewhere else, but here, beneath the noise, beyond the narratives, within the stillness that breathes through all things. To study transcendence is not to study miracles; it is to study what happens when we stop resisting reality and begin to live as its expression.

To understand transcendence through a scientific lens, it is also necessary to look beyond neural activity and molecular shifts into the subtle domains of psychology and meaning. Transcendental states are not merely altered forms of experience—they carry with them a transformation of identity. The person who undergoes such a state often describes a permanent reorientation of self-concept: the loosening of ego-bound narratives, the emergence of unconditional compassion, and the recognition that consciousness is not localised in the body or mind, but unbounded, eternal, and participatory.

This process is well-articulated in the psychology of Carl Jung, who explored the concept of individuation as a journey into wholeness. Jung proposed that the psyche is composed of conscious and unconscious elements. That transcendence occurs when the ego dissolves its claim on centrality and allows the Self, an archetype of totality, to become the guiding force. The symbols and visions that emerge in deep meditation or dream states are not fantasies, but messages from the unconscious, pointing toward integration. In Jungian terms, the mystical experience is the moment when the opposites within the psyche—light and shadow, masculine and feminine, personal and collective—are held in conscious union. In this view, transcendence is not a leap away from the human but a full embrace of it, illumined from within.

In parallel, modern therapeutic modalities such as Internal Family Systems (IFS) and Somatic Experiencing (SE) describe similar territory. These approaches recognise that psychological wounds are not simply cognitive—they are somatic, stored in the body as implicit memory, tension, and energetic fragmentation. When individuals enter deep states of presence—either through breath, ritual, movement, or relational safety—these parts begin to reveal themselves, not to be judged, but to be witnessed and re-integrated. The healing process, then, is not analytical but transcendental—the individual remembers their original coherence not through logic, but through direct experience.

This leads us to a profound insight: transcendence is not the elimination of the self, but the discovery of the self as a field of awareness that contains all aspects of identity without being reduced by any of them. This aligns with the description of non-dual consciousness across various traditions. In *Advaita Vedānta,* it is described as the realisation of the Self as *Brahman.* In Dzogchen, it is the naked awareness that sees without interference. In Christian mysticism, it is the cloud of unknowing, in which God is not grasped by intellect but encountered through surrender. In each case, transcendence is not a break from reality—it is a return to its indivisible source.

From a physiological standpoint, these states often correlate with coherence across multiple systems. Brain imaging studies show increased synchrony between the hemispheres, especially in frontal regions associated with moral reasoning and intuition. Heart rate variability increases, indicating a balance between sympathetic and parasympathetic responses. There is also an emergence of global resonance—a term used in systems theory and biofield science to describe how disparate parts of the body begin to operate in unified rhythm. The subjective feeling of oneness, therefore, has a physiological counterpart: all systems of the body begin to behave as one.

This unity is mirrored in the field of integrative medicine, where spiritual practices are being increasingly incorporated into treatment plans for chronic illness, trauma, and depression. Mindfulness, yoga, energy work, and prayer are no longer viewed as alternative—they are being validated through clinical trials for their ability to reduce pain, enhance mood, and foster healing at the level of meaning. Patients who engage in these practices often report not just symptom relief but a sense of spiritual awakening, even in the face of illness. The suffering becomes a portal—not to despair, but to depth.

One of the most compelling illustrations of this phenomenon is found in near-death experiences (NDEs). Though often controversial, thousands of well-documented cases show consistent features: a sense of leaving the body, entering a realm of light, experiencing unconditional love, and a review of life not in terms of achievement, but in terms of relational impact. Researchers such as Bruce Greyson and Pim van Lommel have compiled rigorous accounts, suggesting that consciousness may persist beyond clinical death and that such experiences often result in lasting personality changes, including greater compassion, reduced fear of death, and a newfound sense of purpose. Whether one interprets NDEs as metaphysical realities or neurochemical phenomena, their transformative impact is undeniable.

Such findings challenge the materialist view that consciousness is merely a product of brain activity. Increasingly, scholars are exploring models in which the brain is not a generator of consciousness, but a receiver or modulator of it, similar to a radio tuning into frequencies. In this framework, spiritual practices do not create transcendence; they fine-tune the instrument, allowing deeper aspects of reality to be perceived. This aligns with the ancient concept of *prāṇa* or life-force energy, which was understood not as a metaphor, but as the medium through which consciousness animates matter.

In cross-cultural terms, this is expressed in many ways. The Sufi mystic speaks of the annihilation of the ego in the Beloved. The Buddhist refers to it as the cessation of suffering through the realisation of emptiness. The Native American refers to the Great Spirit, accessible through vision quests and ceremony. The Kabbalist sees it as devekut—cleaving to the divine. Despite their differences in theology and ritual, these traditions converge on the experience of unity, surrender, and ineffability—the three hallmarks of genuine transcendence.

What science offers today is not the final word, but a bridge—a way to articulate and verify what has always been known in the heart. It provides tools to study the correlates of transcendence, to understand its effects, and to offer it more widely in therapeutic and educational settings. But it must always bow to the mystery it seeks to measure. Transcendence cannot be captured in numbers or charts; it can only be experienced, lived, and shared.

In this light, the future of both science and spirituality may lie not in opposition, but in integration—a world where neuroscientists meditate, physicians pray with patients, classrooms teach silence alongside syllabi, and the lab and the temple are no longer separate. In such a world, knowledge would not compete with wisdom—it would serve it, and the individual, far from being reduced to brain and behaviour, would be recognised for what they are: a bridge between worlds, capable of thought and transcendence, of science and surrender, of knowing and being. In this recognition, the science of transcendence becomes not just a discipline, but a path of remembering that the most advanced system in the universe is not the computer, but the awakened human being.

As this exploration of transcendence draws to a close, a profound and undeniable truth emerges: the human being is wired for the sacred. Whether we approach it through neural patterns, heart rhythms, genetic expression, or meditative insight, all evidence points to the same core realisation — the potential for transcendence is not an anomaly, but a natural function of the integrated self. It is the state in which biology, emotion, and awareness move as one seamless field of presence.

The science of transcendence does not strip away mystery—it restores reverence to the conversation between body and spirit. It affirms that experiences of unity, peace, insight, and unconditional love are not fantasies to be dismissed or domesticated; instead, they are valid dimensions of consciousness, with transformative power and measurable outcomes. The testimonies of mystics across cultures—long viewed as poetic or metaphorical—now find resonance in the language of neurochemistry, epigenetics, and systems theory.

This convergence does not diminish the spiritual; instead, it grounds it. It allows seekers, healers, and scientists to speak a common language—one that honours both data and direct experience, both anatomy and awareness. On this common ground, the soul is no longer treated as superstition, nor is the body seen as mere machinery. Both are understood as expressions of the same field: intelligence in form, energy in motion, and spirit in structure.

What follows from this is a radical reframing of human potential. Suppose transcendence is not the exception but the essence. In that case, education must teach presence, medicine must treat meaning, psychology must honour the soul, and science must be practised with humility, not to conquer nature, but to listen more deeply to its rhythm.

Transcendence, then, becomes a mirror—not of escape, but of integration. It is not about bypassing suffering, but about discovering the light within it. It is not about detaching from life, but about seeing through its veils to what is constant. And this seeing changes everything. It changes how we breathe, how we speak, how we relate, and how we create. It infuses the ordinary with grace, revealing the sacred not in distant heavens, but in the way we hold a cup, a gaze, or a moment.

This is not merely a theory; it is lived, it is seen in the calm of a dying patient who finds peace in prayer, in the steadiness of a monk who meets chaos with compassion, in the laughter of a child immersed in the present, and in the scientist whose awe drives their research more than any hypothesis. These are the fruits of transcendence—not visions, but virtues; not escape, but embodiment; not superiority, but surrender.

In the final analysis, the science of transcendence does not aim to reduce mystery to mechanism. It aims to illuminate the pathways by which the finite touches the infinite, the measurable reveals the unmeasurable, and the self dissolves into the whole. It reminds us that enlightenment is not beyond us. It is encoded within us, waiting to be remembered, honoured, and lived.

And when it is, when the breath becomes still, the mind becomes clear, and the heart becomes vast—then we see, not as the mind sees, but as awareness sees. We see not parts, but patterns; not noise, but harmony; not separation, but oneness. In that moment, the lab becomes a sanctuary, the study becomes a prayer, and the question becomes a doorway—not to answers, but to the presence that transcends all knowing.

This is the frontier where science and spirit meet—not at the edge of knowledge, but at the centre of being.

Chapter 15

Reclaiming the Sacred in a Sensory World

At the heart of every spiritual journey lies a return—not to a distant heaven, but to the immediacy of presence. The path winds through ancient scriptures and modern science, through silence and sound, through touch, breath, memory, and intuition, but it always leads us back to the same place: this body, this breath, this moment. The sacred, it turns out, was never elsewhere. It was always here, embedded in the rhythm of ordinary life, waiting to be remembered.

This remembering is not a mental act—it is a shift in perception. It is seeing with eyes that are no longer distracted, listening with ears that are attuned to subtlety, touching with hands that feel from the soul. It is not about transcending the senses, but inhabiting them more fully and reverently. When we reclaim the sacred in a sensory world, we are not adding something artificial; we are removing what dulls our awareness—the rush, the noise, and the habit of being elsewhere.

We live in an age of overstimulation. Every sense is pulled outward—toward screens, speed, and consumption. The modern world rewards attention that is fractured and constantly shifting. But the cost of this fragmentation is profound: we lose touch with the deep intelligence of the body, the clarity of the breath, the stillness behind thought. We begin to inhabit only the surface of things, forgetting the richness that lives just beneath. Reclaiming the sacred is a radical act of slowing down—choosing presence over distraction, depth over efficiency, and reverence over convenience.

Each of the senses, when honoured, becomes a gateway. The scent of earth after rain can return us to childhood wonder. The taste of food taken with gratitude can become a form of communion. A single breath, followed in and out, can realign the nervous system and calm the mind. The sound of wind in trees, or the space between notes in music, can open the heart to silence. The gaze exchanged with a loved one, when held with awareness, can dissolve the illusion of separation. These are not mystical exceptions but the inherent potential of embodied life when we meet it with presence.

To live this way is to allow the world to become a teacher. The body becomes not only a temple but a text. The senses become not temptations, but tools. The emotions no longer need to be managed or denied—they become guides. Even pain has a place, not as punishment but as a signal, a call inward. Joy, too, is no longer fleeting—it is recognised as the natural expression of undivided awareness. This is not a life of denial, but of fullness. It is not asceticism, but embodiment. It is the merging of form and spirit, where nothing is left out.

And in this merging, the spiritual becomes deeply practical. We begin to see that presence can infuse every action, not just meditation, but washing dishes, walking to work, and greeting a stranger. These moments, once passed over, now become opportunities to practise devotion—not to an external god, but to the sacred pulse within all things. This is the integration the journey points to: not a life removed from the world, but a life woven with presence into the world.

What we reclaim, then, is not just sacredness—it is intimacy, with ourselves, with each other, and with the ground we walk upon. In this intimacy, the boundaries between sacred and secular begin to blur. We see that there was never any separation; every sensation is a potential doorway, every moment is already whole.

To live in this way does not require more time; it only requires more attention. It is not a question of rearranging the outer life, but of transforming the quality of inner participation. It is about bringing the same care to the first sip of tea as to a ritual offering, the same depth to a conversation as to a prayer, and the same awareness to standing in a queue as to standing in a temple. This is the sacred made visible in daily life—not because life has changed, but because we have.

And when enough of us begin to live this way—with clarity, compassion, and embodiment—a subtle transformation ripples outward. The world itself begins to shift. Relationships deepen, spaces become more intentional, and communities become more healing. The earth, long treated as a resource, is once again felt as Mother. In reclaiming the sacred in ourselves, we begin to restore it in the world.

This is the invitation, not to escape, but to return, not to become someone else, but to become more fully who and what we already are: consciousness in form, light in skin, spirit moving through sensation.

Let the body be your altar, let the senses be your scriptures, let each breath be your chant and let every moment be the doorway.

Reclaim the sacred. It has always been yours. When we reclaim the sacred in a sensory world, we are not turning our backs on life—we are finally saying yes to it, yes to its texture, fragrance, nuance, and complexity. We are affirming that enlightenment does not float above the world but breathes within it. That awakening is not a singular event but a daily participation—a choice, moment by moment, to see, to feel, to inhabit. This is not a path of escape, but one of engagement. It is the way of the embodied mystic, the householder yogi, the artist who paints with attention, the parent who listens with presence, the teacher who pauses before speaking.

We often imagine the sacred as something elevated, rare, and set apart. However, in truth, it is often found in the humble and overlooked, such as in the pause between two words, the soft weight of the body resting, the stillness just before dawn, or the way we cradle our face after a difficult day. These moments—simple, sensory, intimate—are no less spiritual than scripture or sanctuary. They are the silent stanzas of a deeper prayer: the prayer of presence.

And presence is always sensory. We do not arrive in the present by thinking about it. We arrive by feeling it—through the body, the breath, the skin, the rhythm. The senses, once trained to rush outward, become instruments of return, drawing us back from abstraction, anxiety, and the projected self, into what is here. This very here, where the air touches the nostrils, where the spine meets the chair, where light moves across a wall. Each detail, seen clearly, becomes a form of grace.

From the beginning of this journey, we have explored how each of the senses offers a thread. Touch teaches presence and intimacy. Sight becomes vision when it sees essence beyond form. Smell evokes memory and spirit. Taste reveals communion and nourishment. Sound opens the space for silence to enter. Breath becomes the rhythm of surrender and aliveness. Intuition, the sixth sense, carries us into the subtler realms. Hormones, memory, and emotion remind us that physiology is not opposed to spirit, but is its canvas. And in the interplay of mind, body, and soul, we have seen how every part of us participates in the sacred.

But participation requires responsibility. It asks us to be stewards of our attention, caretakers of our sensory world. When we rush, numb, consume, or disconnect, we not only harm our system, but we also diminish the sanctity of what could have been a moment of communion. Reclaiming the sacred means choosing again and again to be fully here, to protect our energy not out of withdrawal but to honour its depth. It means treating the world, not as an object, but as a field of mutual presence.

And as we live this way, the ordinary becomes luminous, the simple becomes sufficient. A walk through the trees is no longer a break from life—it is life. Washing the body becomes an act of reverence. Eating a meal becomes a ritual. Touch becomes prayer. Sound becomes guidance. We begin to walk more slowly, speak more deliberately, listen more deeply—not as an effort, but as a natural expression of having come home.

To reclaim the sacred is to reclaim ourselves, to remember that we were never fragmented, only distracted; that we were never impure, only asleep; that the body was never separate from the soul, but its first language; that the senses were never enemies, but invitations.

And as the final note in this journey, let this truth remain: nothing is missing. What you seek is not in some distant future or distant realm. It is in the texture of your breath, the light on your skin, the silence beneath your thoughts. You do not have to become perfect, enlightened, or extraordinary; you have to become present, entirely, gently, consistently. And when you do, you will find that the sacred was never far. It was the taste of your awareness, alive in this moment, waiting to be received.

Conclusion

This is not a conclusion, but a return to the sacred that is already pulsing through your skin, your breath, and your gaze. It is a quiet reminder that enlightenment does not descend from above; it rises gently from within, through the senses you were born with, through the body you already inhabit. To walk this world as if every moment were divine is not idealism—it is truth remembered. And when you live as though the soul speaks through every sensation, you no longer seek the sacred—you become it.

Maa Bhagwati's great grace has reached you with this book. You gave your time to this book. I hope you have gained insight into your mind, intellect, and soul. But I want to tell you one thing: all this would not have been possible without the *Guru's grace*. We are all connected, be it through the universe or something else.

This book stands as a testament to the unwavering support and boundless kindness of Dr. Niharika. Without her, this work would have remained an unfinished dream. Her patience, wisdom, and constant encouragement illuminated every step of this journey. She was there through every challenge — guiding, inspiring, and believing when I doubted myself. More than a mentor, she became the heart behind these pages, ensuring that every idea found its true expression. With deepest gratitude and affection, I dedicate this book to her — for her faith, her effort, and her endless light that made this creation possible."

Maa Bhagwati's great grace has reached you with this book. You gave your time to this book. I hope you have gained insight into your mind, intellect, and soul. But I want to tell you one thing: all this would not have been possible without the Guru's grace. We are all connected, be it through the universe or something else.

सर्व मंगल मांगल्ये शिवे सर्वार्थ साधिके।
शरन्ये त्रयम्बिके गौरी नारायणी नमोस्तुते।।